BUILDING WITH ALTERNATIVES TO LUMBER AND PLYWOOD

NAHB Research Center
Home Builder Press

HOME BUILDER PRESS

Home Builder Press®
National Association of Home Builders
1201 15th Street, NW
Washington, DC 20005-2800

Building with Alternatives to Lumber and Plywood
ISBN 0-86718-392-6

Printed in the United States of America

Library of Congress Cataloging-in-Publication Data

Building with alternatives to lumber and plywood / NAHB Research Center.
p. cm.
Principal author was Eric Lund.
ISBN 0-86718-392-6
1. Building materials--United States--Technological innovations. 2. Building materials industry--United States--Technological innovations. 3. Building--United States--Technological innovations. I. Lund, Eric (Eric M.) II. NAHB Research Center.
TA403.6.B84 1994
691--dc20 93-41672
CIP

For further information, please contact--

Home Builder Press®
National Association of Home Builders
1201 15th Street, NW
Washington, DC 20005-2800

(800) 223-2665

12/93 HBP/AGS 1.5M
10/94 AGS 1.3M R

Acknowledgments

The report on which this publication is based was prepared by the NAHB Research Center through funding provided by the U.S. Department of Housing and Urban Development (HUD). The principal author was Eric Lund, with technical assistance and review provided by Don Luebs, Mark Gibson, and Mark Nowak. Special appreciation is extended to Ron Gebhardt of Gebhardt Associates and William Freeborne of HUD for their guidance and review.

Introduction

Building with Alternatives to Lumber and Plywood identifies a number of alternative materials or building systems that can be used in residential construction under most current building codes, as well as emerging technologies that should be commercially available in the near future. Because most lumber and plywood in residential construction is used for framing and sheathing, the book focuses on alternatives to framing lumber and plywood sheathing for floors, walls, or roofs. The book provides basic information about the properties of various alternatives to conventional lumber and plywood applicable to residential construction.

Though typically more expensive than lumber and plywood, many of the alternative technologies discussed in this book offer certain advantages, such as increased thermal efficiency, fire resistance, or durability. As these technologies find acceptance in the marketplace, their price may become more competitive. Over time, their increased availability and use should help stabilize the supply and cost of essential materials needed for home construction.

To identify and evaluate specific alternatives to lumber and plywood, a search and evaluation was conducted of academic theses and research reports, trade journals, manufacturers' and suppliers' technical and marketing literature, government laboratory research reports and program summaries, and information from the NAHB Research Center's Advanced Housing Technology Program files. Project information and insights also were provided by contacts with manufacturers, designers, engineers, and builders. The last chapter, on wood-saving methods, was drawn from Research Center reports and literature.

Contents

Tables

Figures

Supply, Demand, and Uses of Lumber and Plywood

In most regions of the United States and Canada, wood has long been the predominant building material for residential construction. Satisfactory performance, ready availability, and relatively low cost have made wood the material of choice for most home builders. However, a decreasing supply, particularly of large-dimensioned lumber, threatens the economic stability and cost effectiveness that wood has offered the building industry. Further, expected increases in the price of lumber will undermine housing affordability. Therefore, the housing industry is compelled to consider alternatives to conventional lumber and plywood products.

Pricing information in this book reflects a range of possible prices as estimated in November 1992. Lumber prices have historically been very volatile, largely the result of changes in supply and demand (Figure 1). Therefore, builders are encouraged to check prices with local suppliers.

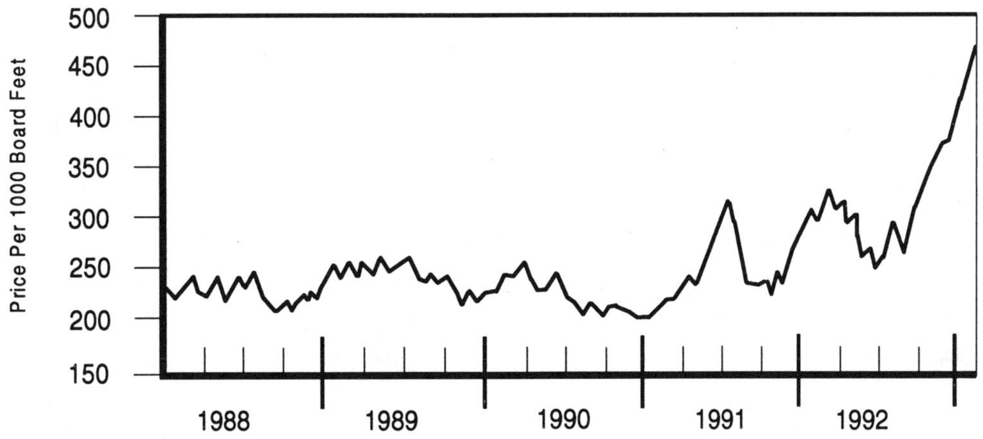

Figure 1. Framing Lumber Composite Price
(Source: Random Lengths, Eugene, OR)

SUPPLY AND DEMAND FOR LUMBER AND PLYWOOD

The declining quality of dimensional lumber reflects what most consider to be a diminishing supply of old-growth timber. Although the amount of standing timber in the United States is actually increasing,[1] it consists primarily of trees planted in the last few decades. While these younger trees grow quickly, they do not provide the long, large-dimensioned lumber that is typically used for joists and rafters. Most of the remaining old-growth forests, which are harvested to produce large-dimensioned lumber and plywood, are located on government-owned land subject to federal regulations.

Several factors affect the supply of and demand for lumber, which in turn affect lumber's price. These include changes in demand of the housing market, the increasing role of federal regulation in determining the amount of land available for professional harvest, duties on lumber imported from Canada, and new design values for the various grades and species of lumber.

The volume of lumber production from publicly-owned lands has declined in the past five years,[2] largely due to the set-asides for the protection of such endangered species as the northern spotted owl. Several other species, including the marbled murrelet on the Pacific coast and the red-cockaded woodpecker, may also become factors in the wood supply. A continuing series of court injunctions, administrative actions, and policy changes is blocking the sale of cutting rights on federal lands. Nonetheless, it takes considerable time before the sale of cutting rights is transformed into logs. It is clear, however, that federal regulation will play an increasing role in determining the amount of federally-owned land available for professional harvest.

A significant share of the lumber consumed by the United States is supplied by Canada. Imports from Canada accounted for 27 percent of 1991 U.S. consumption, down from a peak of 33 percent in 1985.[2] In March 1992, the U.S. government made a preliminary determination that Canadian lumber producers are subsidized by provincial government policies that hold down the cost of timber. In response, the U.S. Department of Commerce called for a countervailing duty of 14.48 percent on Canadian lumber but, in its final determination on May 28, 1992, reduced the duty to 6.51 percent.[3]

In its 1991 *National Design Specification*, the National Forest Products Association (now the American Forest and Paper Association) published new design values for the various grades and species of lumber. The net result in many cases of large-dimensioned lumber was to reduce the allowable design strength and, therefore, spanning capabilities of lumber joists and rafters.

---

[1]Frederick T. Kurpiel, ed., Proceedings of Engineered Wood Products, Processing and Design Conference, sponsored by the North Georgia Chapter of the Southeastern Section of the Forest Products Research Society, Atlanta, GA, March 26-27, 1991.

[2]Michael Carliner and Gopal Ahluwalia, National Association of Home Builders, Economics and Housing Division, Internal memorandum regarding "Lumber Prices" (February 10, 1992).

[3]U.S. Department of Commerce, International Trade Administration, *Federal Register,* May 28, 1992, p. 22570.

Increased building code requirements for earthquake- and hurricane-resistant design will result in increased demand for structural sheathing.

All of these factors tend to place upward pressure on the price of lumber. The long-term rise in lumber prices will, in turn, require harvesters to use the timber supply efficiently and prompt changes by manufacturers, designers, and builders.

USES OF LUMBER AND PLYWOOD

Throughout the United States, wood remains the dominant material for home building—well over 90 percent of new single-family homes are framed with wood (Table 1). In addition, the amount of lumber consumed by the repair and remodeling markets has increased substantially since 1982, accounting for an estimated one-third of the lumber purchased in the United States in 1991. This market has become significantly more important over the past decade as the stock of older houses has increased. Almost 39 percent of all single-family houses were built before 1940.

Table 1
Construction Materials in New Homes

	Material	Single-Family Detached	Single-Family Attached	Multifamily Low-Rise
Exterior Wall	Wood Framing	94%	92%	89%
	Steel Framing	0%	0%	1%
	Concrete Block	5%	8%	5%
	Other	1%	0%	5%
Interior Wall	Wood Framing	98%	96%	84%
	Steel Framing	1%	3%	6%
	Other	1%	1%	10%

Source: Adapted from Residential Product Demand New Construction Report, F.W. Dodge Residential Statistics Services, Lexington, MA, 1990.

Collectively, residential construction consumes approximately two-thirds of the lumber used by the construction industry. The balance is used in commercial or nonbuilding construction (Table 2).

Table 2
U.S. Consumption of Softwood Lumber

	1986	1987	1988	1989	1990
Construction					
New Residential (new housing)	44%	42%	40%	39%	36%
Repair and Remodeling	26%	26%	27%	27%	29%
New Nonresidential	7%	8%	8%	8%	8%
All Other	23%	24%	25%	26%	27%
Total	**100%**	**100%**	**100%**	**100%**	**100%**

Source: National Association of Home Builders, Washington, DC, 1990.

Table 3 displays lumber use in new homes by type of application. The subtotals point out that nearly 85 percent of the wood used to construct a home is used for framing. The nonframing uses of wood are primarily siding and trim. Wood siding and trim alternatives currently enjoy fairly high market shares; vinyl/aluminum siding, brick, stucco, and plastic lumber are readily available substitutes, some even offering the advantage of lower initial costs.

Table 3
Use of Lumber by Component
(board feet)

		Single-Family Detached		**Single-Family Attached**		**Multifamily Low-Rise**	
Framing Lumber by Application	Floors	2,185		1,261		1,265	
	Interior Walls	2,083		2,428		1,194	
	Exterior Walls	2,400		1,175		834	
	Roofs	4,104		2,030		2,070	
	Detached Garages and Carports	260		154		341	
	Subtotal	11,032	(84%)	7,048	(86%)	5,704	(86%)
Nonframing		2,096	(16%)	1,147	(14%)	910	(14%)
Total		**13,128**		**8,195**		**6,614**	

Source: Residential Product Demand New Construction Report, F.W. Dodge Residential Statistics Services, Lexington, MA, 1991.

Table 4 shows average sheathing use in new homes. Although plywood is the predominant structural sheathing, nonveneer panels such as oriented strand board (OSB) continue to gain market share.

Table 4
Structural Sheathing Panel Use in 1990 New Homes
(per house by square feet)

Sheathing Product	Single-Family Detached	Single-Family Attached	Multifamily Low-Rise
Plywood*	4,278	2,811	1,654
Nonveneer Panels* (OSB, waferboard, particleboard)	2,637	1,225	1,022

* Reduced to 3/8-inch equivalents.
Source: Residential Product Demand New Construction Report, F.W. Dodge Residential Statistics Services, Lexington, MA, 1991.

According to the American Plywood Association (APA), sheathing can be manufactured in a variety of ways—as plywood (cross-laminated wood veneer), composites (veneer faces bonded to reconstituted wood cores), or nonveneer panels (OSB). By broadening the range of panel configurations and compositions, APA performance-rated panels allow raw materials to be used more efficiently.

Performance-rated veneer panels, nonveneer panels, and composite panels are all manufactured under the provisions of a standard developed by the plywood industry through the U.S. Department of Commerce.[4] APA-associated mills rate their sheathing products by performance rather than by thickness of material type. APA performance-rated panels are easy to use and specify because the recommended end use and maximum support spacings are clearly indicated in the APA trademark. Thickness is not a reliable indicator since many factors, including wood species, number of plies, and manufacturing methods, all affect strength.

As of late 1992, only one company manufactured a composite panel rated for structural use. This panel has plywood veneers both on the outer faces and in the center, with wood fiber compressed in between. It is distributed primarily on the west coast.

[4]U.S. Product Standard PS 2-92, Performance Standard for Wood-Based Structural Use Panels.

Table 5
Alternatives to Lumber and Plywood (commercially available)

Alternative	Definition	Building Component	Advantages	Disadvantages
Engineered Wood	Products combining wood veneers or fibers with adhesives to form products of uniformly high quality and strength	Structural frame and sheathing	Increased quality and consistency; efficient use of wood; design flexibility	Higher cost; lack of industry standards
a Glue-Laminated Lumber	Laminated sawn lumber, stacked and bonded with adhesives	Beams, headers, and columns	Can be manufactured with camber	
b Laminated Veneer Lumber (LVL)	Layers of thin veneers adhered, pressed, and cured	Beams, headers, columns, and joists	Strength	
c Parallel Strand Lumber	Long, narrow strands of wood adhered under pressure and cured with microwave heat	Beams, headers, and columns	Strength and appearance	
d I-Beams	Solid or LVL flanges grooved to receive OSB or plywood webs	Headers, joists, and rafters	Speed of construction	
e Oriented Strand Board (OSB)	Strands of wood aligned in cross-laminated layers	Roof and wall sheathing, subflooring	Price	Swelling from moisture
Laminated Fiberboard Structural Sheathing	Fibrous plies laminated under pressure and covered with foil or polyethylene	Wall sheathing	Low air infiltration	Strength may be inadequate under high winds or seismic forces
Light-Gauge Structural Steel	Galvanized steel framing components as a direct substitute for conventional wood-framing systems	Floor, wall, and roof systems	Non-combustibility; durability; consistent quality; supply/pricing stability; strength	Lack of familiarity; required engineering analysis; thermal performance
Structural Foam Sandwich Panels	Structural panel consisting of two stiff skins separated by a foam core	Wall and roof systems	Thermal performance; speed of construction; strength	Interfacing with other trades; insect infestation; overheating roof shingles
Concrete Systems				
a Insulated Concrete Wall Forms	Concrete cast between two foam panels or into the hollow cores of stackable, interlocking insulation blocks	Wall systems	Speed of construction; extends construction season	Extra care required during casting
b Insulated Concrete Wall System	Concrete cast over a polystyrene board in the center of conventional forms	Wall systems	Fire resistance; durability	Increased labor
c Welded-Wire Sandwich Panels	Shotcrete applied over a steel-reinforced foam panel	Wall and roof systems	Speed of construction; fire resistance; durability	Required structural analysis
Conventional Concrete Block	Mixture of cement, aggregate, and water compacted and cured into blocks	Wall systems	Noncombustible; durable; readily available	Additional insulation required in most conditions
Insulated Concrete Block	Conventional block cores filled with either plastic inserts or foam insulation	Wall systems	Speed of construction	Some systems require structural analysis
Structural Light-Weight Concrete	Use of admixtures and/or light-weight aggregates with conventional concrete	Wall systems	Speed of construction	

ALTERNATIVE MATERIALS

The alternatives that are discussed in the following chapters are summarized in Table 5. Products distributed to most regions of the country were considered; however, this list is not all-inclusive. Alternatives applicable to or available only in selected regions of the country are not discussed. Examples of alternatives not mentioned include adobe and rammed earth, both of which are regional vernaculars that reflect specific earth-building traditions, and Comply™, a structural sheathing panel available only on the west coast. The alternatives discussed in subsequent chapters are organized around the following framework:

- **Product, material, or method description.** A figure accompanies the product description in each section of the report. Sections of the figure are darkened to identify where in the home the alternative is used.

- **Advantages and disadvantages.** Advantages and disadvantages are discussed in terms of function (performance, use, and quality) and productivity.

- **Installation.** Information is provided on important installation details.

- **Cost estimate.** Where possible, manufacturer list prices or estimated ranges of installation costs are provided. These costs are based on information from various manufacturers, distributors, and builders and do not include any builder mark-ups (such as profit and overhead). The information does not represent a definitive study on costs but, rather, is intended to provide a range of costs. These reflect costs in late November 1992, and should be confirmed with local suppliers.

Advantages and disadvantages specific to individual products are discussed in each section of the report. However, all of the products face institutional barriers that can be collectively addressed. With few exceptions, the products presented in this report do not enjoy the advantage of lower initial costs compared to lumber. Because the average size of firms in the home building industry is small, incorporating an alternative that is not cost-effective can be risky. In addition, builders may be unfamiliar with the product, introducing a learning curve and slowing production. Further, local building officials can play a large role in controlling the rate at which local builders adopt alternative materials and methods.

In addition to presenting specific alternatives to wood, methods for saving wood in conventional construction are noted in the last chapter.

Engineered Wood Products

Engineered wood products (EWPs) represent a new class of structural wood members that have evolved over the last two decades and are commercially available today. EWPs combine wood veneers and fibers with adhesives into beams, headers, joists, panels, and other products of uniformly high quality and strength.

EWPs address the lumber industry's most pressing problem—supply—by making efficient use of material once considered unsuitable, such as wood from smaller trees and inferior species. As wood resources diminish, whether by professional harvest or government-imposed logging restrictions, the transition to EWPs is helping to sustain wood's competitive position in residential construction.

The story of these products is largely the story of adhesives. Advances in adhesive technology over the past 50 years have made possible a wide variety of composites. Phenol-formaldehyde and urea-formaldehyde resins are the most common adhesives. The waterproof phenolics are the resin of choice for structural-use products but are more expensive than the urea resins. Also, some mills are beginning to use methylene diphenyl isocyanate (MDI) and polymeric MDI (PMDI) adhesives. Although the primary advantage of the isocyanate adhesives is a shorter press time, manufacturers claim that use of the glue results in a finished product with increased dimensional stability and less outgassing than one adhered with formaldehydes.

ADVANTAGES AND DISADVANTAGES

The entire class of EWPs displays some advantages and disadvantages, although not all products reflect all characteristics. These are discussed collectively followed by a discussion of each EWP, its unique advantages and disadvantages, if any, and present installation and cost information specific to the product.

Advantages

- **Increased quality and consistency.** The manufacturing process of most EWPs removes or disperses weaknesses such as knots and reassembles the wood material into a high-quality product with more uniform structural properties than solid lumber (Table 6). In addition, the components of EWPs are uniformly dried (usually to 8 to 12 percent moisture content) before they are compressed and adhered into their final shape. The relatively low moisture content provides predictable, consistent physical characteristics from piece to piece. Kiln-dried lumber, by contrast, is dried to a 15 to 19 percent moisture content, and therefore more prone to shrinking and warping. Wood in buildings usually reaches equilibrium at about 12 percent moisture content, depending on the region of the country and the degree of interior conditioning.

Table 6
Relative Strengths of Wood Products

	Design Values in Pounds per Square Inch					
	Fiber Stress in Bending	Tension Parallel to Grain	Shear Parallel to Grain	Compression Perpendicular to Grain	Compression Parallel to Grain	Modulus of Elasticity
Parallel Strand Lumber[1]	2,950	2,400	290	600	2,900	2,000,000
Laminated Veneer Lumber[2]	2,875	1,850	285	500	2,700	2,000,000
Glue Laminated Lumber	1,600 to 2,400	650 to 1,300	90 to 200	300 to 600	900 to 1,750	1,100,000 to 1,800,000
Southern Pine, select structural KD, 2x10	2,050	1,100	90	565	1,850	1,800,000
Southern Pine No 2, KD, 2x10	1,050	575	90	565	1,500	1,600,000
Spruce-Pine-Fir (South) No 2, KD, 2x10	825	357	70	335	975	1,100,000

[1]Parallam PSL, 2x10
[2]Micro=Lam, 2x10

Source: Product literature and the 1991 NFPA *National Design Specification.*

- **Efficient use of wood.** Newer manufacturing techniques make better use of existing trees by incorporating up to 80 percent of the incoming log into the final product.[1] By contrast, typical sawmills recover about 50 percent of the original log, of which only about 15 percent is high-grade lumber.

- **Design flexibility.** EWPs can be produced in widths, depths, and, especially, beam lengths that are not otherwise feasible. The manufacturing, joining, and laminating

[1]Phil McCafferty, "Reinventing Wood," *Popular Science,* May 1990, p. 96.

methods used in EWP production give designers the freedom to specify longer spans without the need for intermediate supports.

- **Appearance.** Because some EWPs have a pronounced grain-like pattern (an appearance some home buyers find more desirable than common framing lumber), the members can be exposed. The products' appearance can change depending on how they are cut and whether they are intended for staining and finishing.

Disadvantage

- **Lack of industry standards.** Because of different proprietary production methods, products even within the same general category vary widely. Each EWP has its own characteristics, which makes it difficult to draw comparisons.

GLUE-LAMINATED LUMBER

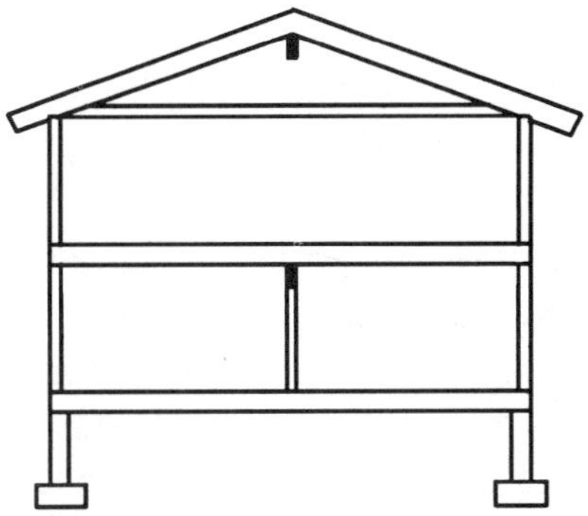

Engineered wood first emerged in the 1950s with the advent of glue-laminated beams, columns, and arches. Glue-laminated members consist of 1x or 2x lumber that is glued in stacks to the desired shape and size. The individual laminations may also be end-joined with adhesives to provide continuous lengths. As a result, virtually any length and depth can be obtained. Nonetheless, the production of glue-laminated lumber relies on solid sawn lumber and traditional milling techniques, which recover about only 50 percent of the individual log.

Glue-laminated beams are manufactured to a national standard (ANSI, AITC A190.1-1983) that has been accepted by all three United States model building codes.

Advantages

- **Strength.** During assembly, laminations are arranged by the grade of lumber, with the higher-quality grades placed on the outer portions of the beam in higher-stress zones. The members are specified by the required mechanical properties as well as by appearance (Table 6).

- **Camber.** Beams can be manufactured either straight or with a camber to offset dead-load deflection. Curved members in vaulted configurations have spanned over 500 feet.

Installation

Practically all manufacturers of engineered wood products provide technical support, including span charts and installation details. Recently, some manufacturers have been marketing members with 3½- and 5½-inch widths designed to accommodate conventional framing dimensions. Stock members are also available; however, the widths of these members are typically 3⅛- and 5⅛- inches, slightly narrower than 2x4 and 2x6 framing material. Connections are usually made with readily available nailed clips and hangers. Bolted gussets and brackets are required for heavy loads. For beams that remain exposed, connections can be custom made.

Cost Estimate

Based on estimates from distributors, a nominal 4x12 glue-laminated member costs $4.00 to $5.50 per lineal foot; a nominal 6x12 member costs $8.75 to $9.00 per lineal foot.

LAMINATED VENEER LUMBER (LVL)

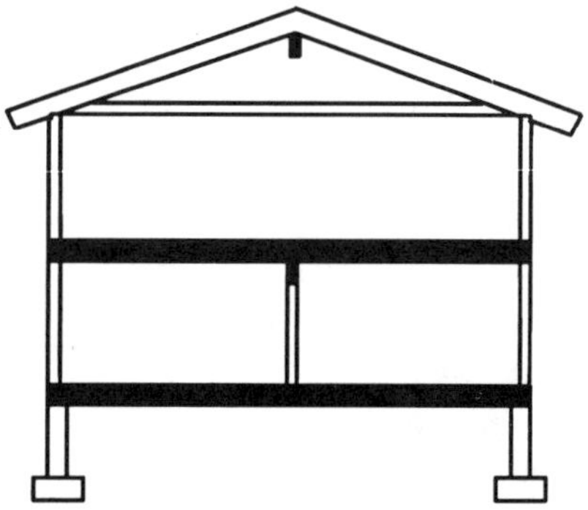

Even though laminated veneer lumber (LVL) was first used in the 1940s for high-strength aircraft parts, commercial production of LVL for high-grade structural members did not start until 1971. Today, several manufacturers use similar processes to produce LVL, which is used for headers, beams, columns, joists, and as flanges for wood I-beams. The Council of American Building Officials (CABO) has issued National Evaluation Reports that provide the basis for building code approval for LVL.[2]

The manufacturing process is similar to that for plywood. Logs, usually Douglas fir or southern pine, are peeled on a lathe into veneer panels that are usually about 1/8- or 1/10-inch thick. However, while plywood veneers are cross-laminated, LVL is produced with its veneers layered parallel to one other. After the veneers are coated with a waterproof adhesive, they are bonded by heat and pressure. The end-joints are staggered, resulting in a continuous billet of lumber up to 1¾ inches thick and 4-feet wide. The billet is then cut to the desired widths. Some manufacturers offer thicker members by gluing together two or more of the 1¾-inch billets.

---

[2] J. Dobbin McNatt and Russell C. Moody, "Structural Composite Lumber," *Progressive Architecture*, December 1990, p. 34.

Advantages

- **Strength.** LVL is capable of long spans, thereby increasing design flexibility (Table 6).

A 1-3/4-inch by 9-1/2-inch laminated veneer lumber sample.

Installation

The most common LVL material is the 1¾-inch-wide billet. The billet can be used individually for repetitive members such as joists, or it can be built up on site for use as headers and beams. The clips, hangers, and connectors used with LVL are readily available and used much like conventional hardware.

As with other engineered wood products, LVL is manufactured to a lower moisture content than solid lumber and therefore reaches equilibrium at the job site at a different rate than solid lumber. Consequently, in some cases solid lumber and LVL should not be used together as joists in the same floor assembly.

LVL must be sized for specific load conditions and cannot be used as a standard material. The manufacturer or distributor sizes the LVL at no added cost.

Manufacturers provide specific procedures for site-built LVL beams. It is important to refer to manufacturers' recommendations for nailing and bolting schedules for built-up beams.

Much like any girder, header, or beam, LVL beams should not be drilled or notched for electrical and plumbing pass-throughs. Because LVL is manufactured to a low moisture content and will most likely absorb moisture as it is transported to the site and installed, manufacturers stress the importance of covering LVL from the weather and storing it on blocks at the site.

Cost Estimate

Based on estimates provided by distributors, nominal 2x12 LVL costs $2.50 to $4.00 per lineal foot.

PARALLEL STRAND LUMBER

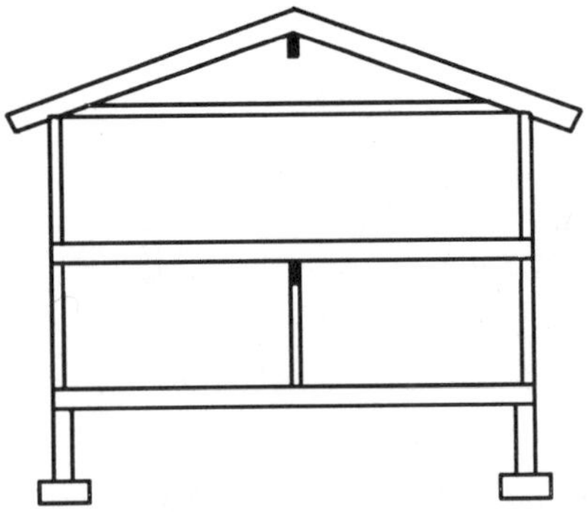

The newest category of EWP, parallel strand lumber (PSL) has been available in the United States since about 1990. PSL was invented in 1969 but underwent 19 years of research and development before it was commercialized in Canada in 1988. PSL is used for beams, columns, and headers. The manufacturer claims that pressure-treated PSL is also available for exterior applications.

At the outset, the PSL production process resembles the LVL production process in that incoming logs are debarked and peeled into thin veneers. At this point, however, the PSL process clips the veneers into ½-inch-wide strands. These strands are then combined with adhesives and cured under pressure with microwave-generated heat to form large billets 12 inches wide by 17 inches deep and up to 66 feet long. The billets are then sawn to specific sizes.

A 4x12 (nominal) parallel strand lumber sample.

Advantages

- **Strength.** Much like LVL, the design values of PSL allow long spans and more design flexibility (Table 6).

- **Appearance.** PSL's pronounced grain pattern is an appearance some home buyers find attractive.

Installation

PSL is available in widths ranging from 1¾ to 7 inches; two plies of the 2-11/16-inch-thick members match 5½-inch walls. Most connections for engineered lumber beams are similar to those used for conventional framing. However, given that PSL beams can support higher loads than solid lumber beams, a greater bearing area may be required. The manufacturer can provide tables outlining the required bearing lengths.

Sideloading or hanging joists on only one side of the beam is not recommended for multiple plies unless engineered connections have been provided. But because PSL is available in large widths, on-site construction of built-up beams can be avoided. Much like LVL, PSL should not be drilled or notched and should be stored on site according to manufacturers' recommendations to avoid swelling problems.

Cost Estimate

Based on estimates provided by distributors, a nominal PSL 4x12 costs $5.00 to $7.50 per lineal foot.

I-BEAMS

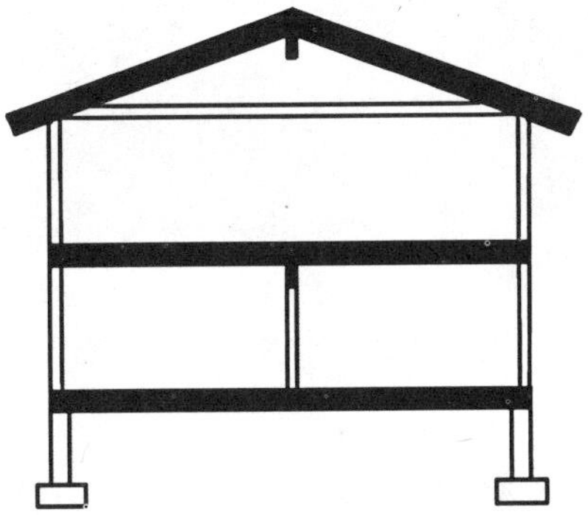

Now produced by a variety of manufacturers, wood I-beams are typically made from 2x4 machine-stressed lumber or LVL flanges grooved to receive an OSB or plywood web that is glued in place. I-beams are available in widths up to 7 inches, depths up to 30 inches, and lengths up to 66 feet, and are typically used as headers, floor joists, and rafters.

Even though I-beam design is similar among fabricators, each manufacturer uses its own proprietary process. Variations among manufacturers relate to production techniques, patented joints for the flange-web connection, types of adhesives, and the grade and types of flange and web material. An American Society for Testing and Materials standard (ASTM D5055-90) that lists common criteria for I-beams was approved and published in July 1990. This standard provides accepted measures for the industry-wide development of design values and quality control. Manufacturers formulate their own design and materials to meet the performance specifications, which include criteria for vertical loads, lateral bracing, joist depth and spacing, and deflection.

Advantages

- **Speed of construction.** Advocates claim that I-beams lower construction costs by reducing the labor needed to erect the beams. In fact, the deeper joists can span the entire width of a house and thereby halve the number of joists to be handled. Given their light weight (about 2 pounds per lineal foot), the beams are easy to manage. Some I-beams have prescored knockout holes for plumbing and electrical lines.

A 12-inch deep (nominal) wood I-beam sample.

- **Dimensional stability.** The flanges of I-beams typically are made of LVL or machine stress-rated lumber and thus are very straight regardless of length.

Installation

While manufacturers' installation guides provide complete details and span tables, the installation of I-beams can be handled with conventional nails, tools, and readily available metal connectors. Much like other engineered wood products, I-beams are manufactured to a lower moisture content than solid lumber and therefore reach equilibrium at the job site at a different rate than does solid lumber. Consequently, I-beams and solid lumber should not be used together as joists or rafters in the same floor or roof assembly.

Web stiffeners or blocks normally are used at bearing points to help reduce the load on the flange-web connection, especially in the case of deeper joists (Figure 2). Web stiffeners also are required where hangers do not offer lateral support of the joist's top flange (Figure 3). In general, nails driven into the stiffeners should not exceed the diameter of a 16d nail. Nails driven into the flanges should not exceed the diameter of a 10d nail or be longer than 1½ inches.

Large-diameter holes can be drilled in the webbing for ducts, but the flange material cannot be cut. Manufacturers provide recommendations on drilling limits; some joists are available prepunched.

Cost Estimate

Based on estimates provided by distributors, the I-beam equivalent of a nominal 2x12 costs $1.00 to $1.50 per lineal foot.

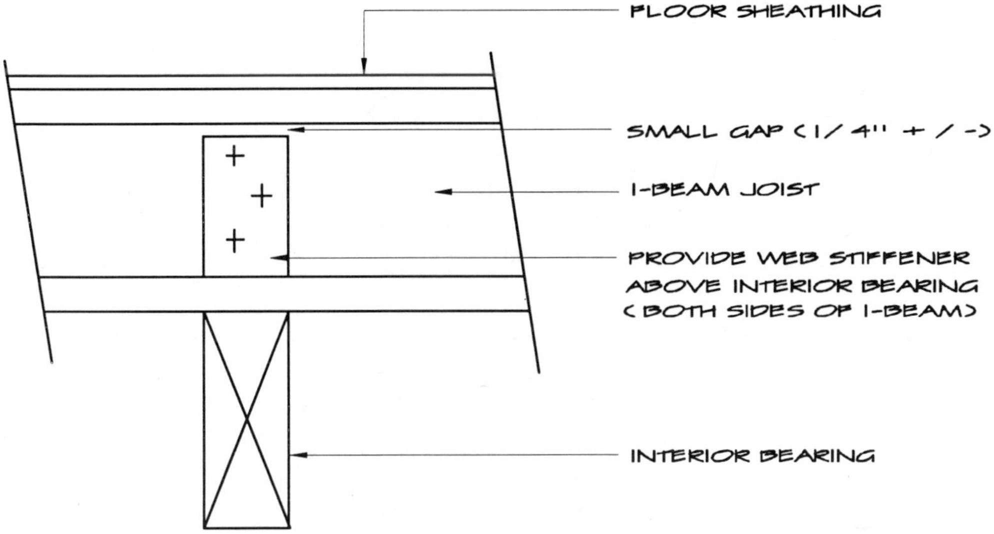

Figure 2. Wood I-Beam Stiffener

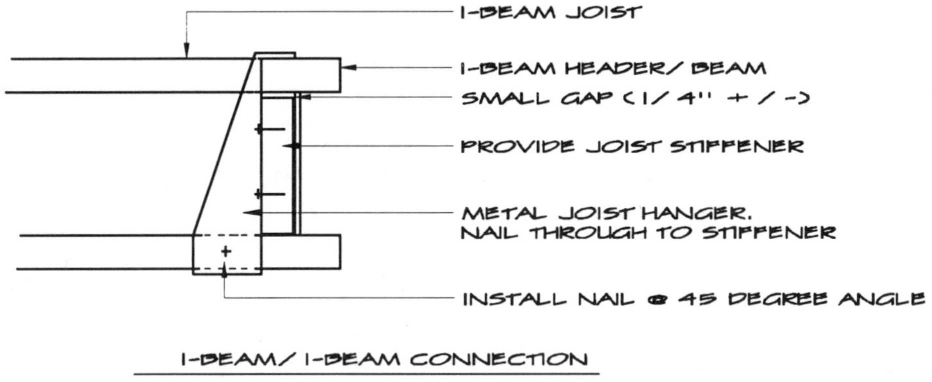

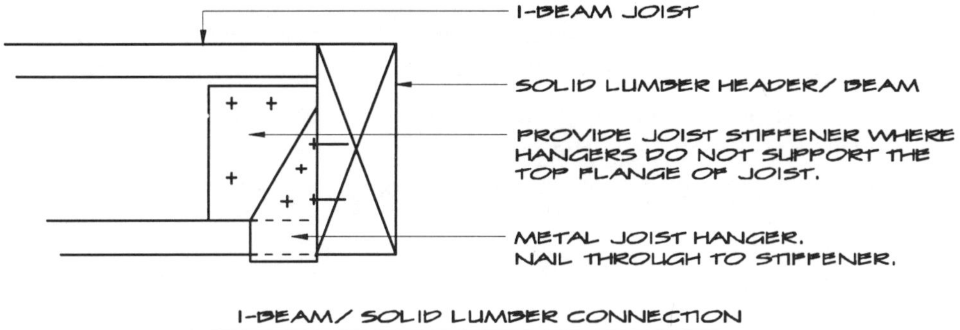

Figure 3. I-Beam/Stiffener/Steel Connector Detail

ORIENTED STRAND BOARD (OSB)

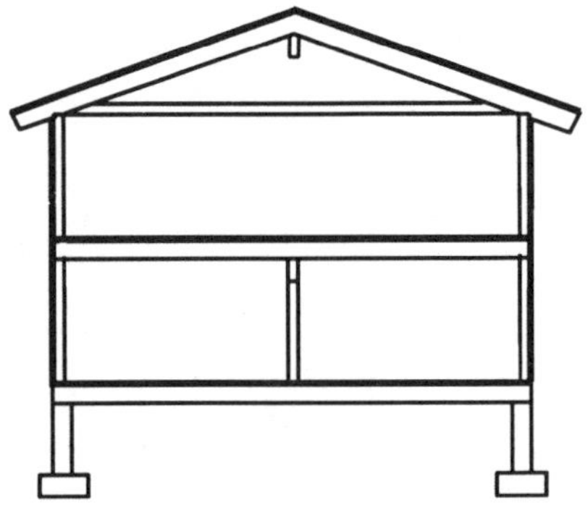

Oriented strand board has been commercially available for about 10 years. Initial resistance to OSB was largely the result of the poor image created by some of the product's low-quality particleboard predecessors. But, today, OSB is widely accepted and used for roof and wall sheathing, subflooring, siding, and as webs for wood I-beams.

As for the manufacturing process, logs are first cut into strands; aspen and other low-density woods are preferred because they are easy to cut into long strands parallel to the grain. Board strength is largely a function of species and strand length—the longer the strand, the stronger the board. The strands are then blended with a resin and mechanically oriented in layers. The face layers are oriented parallel with the long dimension; the core with the short dimension. The panel is then compressed to its final thickness.

Disadvantages

- **Swelling.** Because OSB is manufactured to a 2 to 5 percent moisture content[3] as opposed to about 6 percent for plywood, it absorbs more moisture in reaching equilibrium.

- **Exposure rating.** Even though OSB uses the same glue as exterior grade plywood, it is not designed for applications subject to permanent exposure to the elements.

Installation

OSB panels are available in sizes similar to that of plywood (typically 4 feet by 8 feet), although sizes up to 8 feet by 24 feet are also available. Because OSB is prone to swelling, manufacturers recommend gapping the panels by ⅛ inch at the ends and by ⅛ inch along the edges. While proper spacing eliminates potential buckling problems for walls and roofs, underlayment may be required over OSB subfloors depending on the finish floor material. Further, the use of OSB near potential plumbing and fixture leaks should be considered. Nails can be driven as close as ¼ inch from the panel edges without breaking out. Except under high-loading situations, the same nailing schedules that apply to plywood also apply to OSB.

[3] Charles Wardell, "Composition Panels," *Fine Homebuilding*, April-May 1991, p. 78.

Cost Estimate

OSB is less expensive to manufacture than plywood because it is made from abundant, fast-growing trees. Plywood relies on larger, higher quality "peeler" logs. Based on estimates provided by distributors, OSB costs $0.25 to $0.30 per square foot.

INFORMATION SOURCES

Additional information on engineered wood products can be obtained from:

American Forest and Paper Association
1250 Connecticut Avenue, NW, Suite 200
Washington, DC 20036
(202) 463-2700

American Plywood Association
Post Office Box 11700
Tacoma, WA 98411
(206) 565-6600

Laminated Fiberboard Structural Sheathing

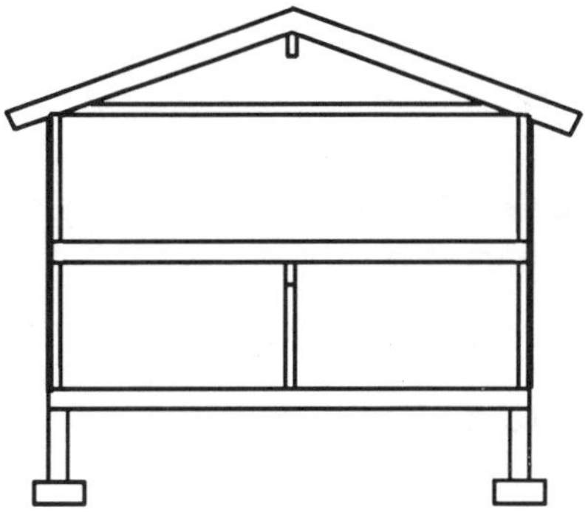

Fiberboard sheathings are light-weight panels made from wood or agricultural by-products. "Blackboard" fiberboard sheathing, produced in a process similar to paper but without the final pressing, is impregnated with emulsified asphalt. It is commonly used with a structural-use panel on the corners for racking strength. Laminated fiberboards, on the other hand, are recognized for lateral bracing in some local jurisdictions, without the need for a structural-use panel or other corner bracing.

Laminated fiberboard sheathing has been available for over 30 years. The panels consist of fibrous plies laminated under pressure and covered with aluminum foil or polyethylene. The panels provide racking strength and weather resistance when used as wall sheathing. Two manufacturers have obtained listings from the three model building codes for their laminated fiberboard sheathing products (refer to CABO Report No NER-298 and ICBO Evaluation Report No 1439).

Advantages

- **Low air infiltration.** Because the laminated fiberboard is pliable and thin (thicknesses range from 0.085 inches to 0.137 inches), the panels can be lapped at the joints to create a uniform seal.

Disadvantages

- **Strength.** Laminated fiberboard sheathing can provide the racking strength required by many local codes, although in areas with high lateral loads due to wind or seismic forces, additional bracing may be required. All of the panels have a maximum allowable frame spacing, typically either 16 inches or 24 inches on center. In addition, laminated fiberboard sheathing does not provide a nail base; therefore, the siding must be nailed directly to the framing studs.

Installation

Typically the manufacturers require a fastener spacing schedule of 3 inches at panel edges and 6 inches at intermediate supports. However, manufacturers or local codes should be consulted to determine the appropriate spacing for a given product. Suggested fastener types include 1¼-inch long 11-gauge galvanized roofing nails, and 16-gauge galvanized staples with a 7/16-inch crown and 1¼-inch legs. The panels are available in 8-foot by 8-foot sheets and can be cut with a utility knife. To prevent buckling, the joints should either be lapped or installed with a 1/16-inch gap.

Cost Estimate

Based on estimates provided by distributors, laminated fiberboard sheathing costs $0.11 to $0.20 per square foot.

INFORMATION SOURCES

Additional information on Laminated Fiberboard Structural Sheathing can be obtained from:

Fiber-Lam, Inc
Post Office Box 135
Doswell, VA 23047
(804) 876-3135

Simplex Products Division
Post Office Box 10
Adrian, MI 49221
(517) 263-8881

Steel Framing

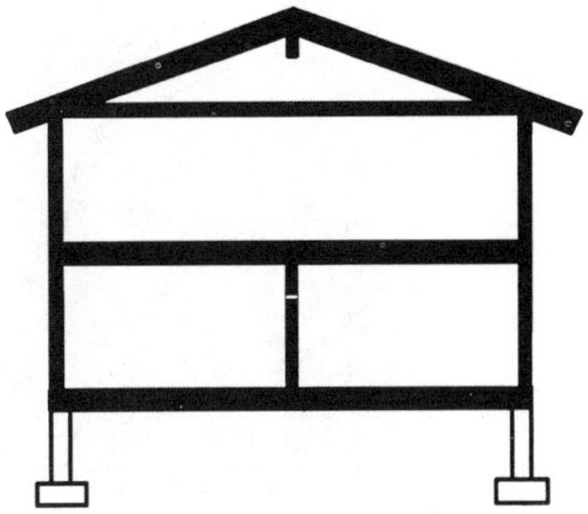

Steel construction in the United States is commonly associated with commercial, institutional, and industrial buildings. For these buildings, conditions of strength, noncombustibility, and design versatility have been more economically achieved by using steel and concrete. The residential building industry can, however, also benefit from the advantages of steel. In Japan, for example, more than one-third of homes started in 1987 were built with steel framing systems.

While most residential steel framing manufacturers in the United States currently target the multifamily high-density markets, they also produce several systems designated for single-family detached homes. Also, because of their light weight, steel systems could see a growth in market share of prefabricated systems. With the great need for housing abroad (in Israel, Mexico, and Poland, for example), the United States prefabricated housing industry could be revamped and expanded to employ steel framing.

In virtually all homes, including those framed with wood, steel framing can be used for certain components such as roof trusses, interior partition walls, and soffits. Nonload-bearing interior partition walls are discussed in the installation section.

Advantages

- **Noncombustible.** Steel is noncombustible, which may result in lower insurance premiums for the home buyer.

- **Durability.** Steel is not susceptible to rot or termites; it does not shrink, warp, or swell. Galvanized steel resists corrosion.

- **Consistent quality.** Galvanized steel studs are manufactured in the quality-controlled setting of the factory. The prepunching of studs provides a consistent cut-out for electrical and plumbing lines.

Single-family residence framed with light-gauge steel.

- **Supply and pricing stability.** Because the steel manufacturing industry can rely on a relatively stable resource base, it does not experience the price volatility that characterizes the lumber market.

- **Strength.** Steel framing manufacturers suggest that steel's high-strength-to-weight ratio—combined with the use of framing screws that resist uplifting loads more effectively than nails—produces a structure that performs better than conventional wood construction during earthquakes and hurricanes. However, while steel framing manufacturers offer an engineered and well-detailed structure that should perform well when subjected to earthquake and hurricane loads, steel framing has yet to establish a performance record.

Disadvantages

- **Lack of familiarity.** Building officials, engineers, and architects need to be educated about steel framing systems' capabilities as they apply to residential construction; the work force needs to be trained in the use of the systems.

- **Required engineering analysis.** Manufacturers of steel framing systems offer engineering analysis as part of their package. Nonetheless, builders need to develop familiarity with the capabilities of these systems.

- **Thermal performance.** Because thermal bridging is increased by the high thermal conductivity of steel, questions regarding the thermal performance of steel-framed houses remain unanswered. CABO's 1989 Model Energy Code shows that the conductivity of a wall framed with steel is up to 110 percent higher than that of a comparable wall framed with wood. In addition, the June 1992 draft of the ASHRAE Proposed Standard 90.2 includes parallel path correction factors ranging from 0.45 to 0.60 for wall frames that contain metal stud assemblies.

Installation

Steel framing can be installed in much the same way that wood framing is installed. Both steel and wood use a typical 16- or 24-inch on center stud framing system. Therefore, incor- porating steel into residential con- struction should not involve systemic change to construction methods. None of the independent trades (framers, plumbers, electricians) needs to alter current practice drastically. Further, the stud framing system can be deployed either on site or with panels prefabricated off site. Although a learning curve is associated with any new material, the specifications and qualities of steel components are probably easier to understand than the section properties, grades, and species of wood products. A brief description of common framing components follows.

Installation of steel framing.

- **Structural "C" (Figure 4).** The "C" is the predominant shape used for floor joists, wall studs, roof rafters, and ceiling joists. Standard dimensions are nearly identical to those of dimension lumber, with flange widths about 1½ inches and web depths that range from 2 to 12 inches. Gauges ranging from 12 to 22 can be ordered. Studs used in typical load-bearing applications are 16 to 20 gauge. The "C" is available both prepunched and unpunched.

- **Track (or channel) (Figure 5).** Track is commonly used for rim joists, top and bottom plates, and blocking. It is normally specified in the same gauge as the framing material with which it is used. Track is available both prepunched and unpunched.

- **Angle (Figure 6).** Angle can be used as a ledger or a connection bracket or for stiffening, bracing, or blocking.

- **Cold rolled and hat channel (Figure 7).** Similar in shape and gauge to track, the smaller-sized channel is used for stiffening, bracing, and blocking. Hat channel is used for furring.

- **Cold rolled zee (Figure 8).** The zee can be used in structural applications as a roof purlin or in lighter gauges for furring.

All members are fastened with screws. Typically, a ½-inch-long, low-profile, zinc-coated, pan head screw is used. To protect electrical wiring, plastic grommets are required at all penetrations of the steel framing. Figure 9 shows several built-up beam details and Figure 10 a steel framed wall section.

Nonload-bearing interior partition walls can be constructed by using one of two methods: tilt-up construction or the installation of top and bottom tracks that are "filled in" with wall studs. An interior partition wall is shown in Figure 10.

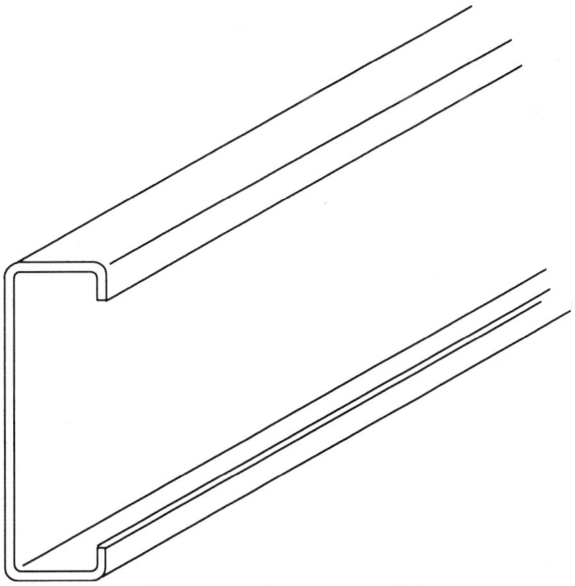

Figure 4. Structural "C"

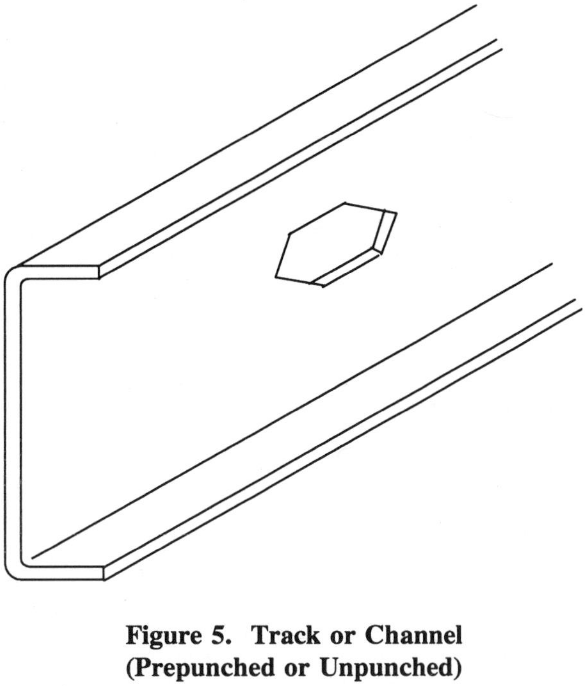

Figure 5. Track or Channel
(Prepunched or Unpunched)

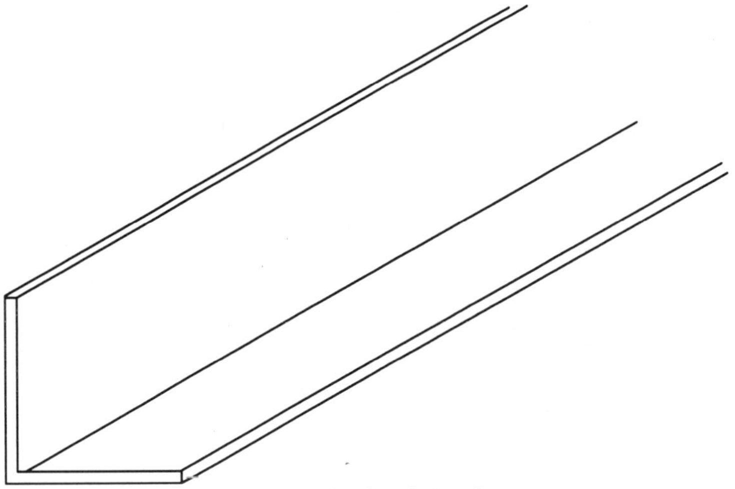

Figure 6. Steel Angle

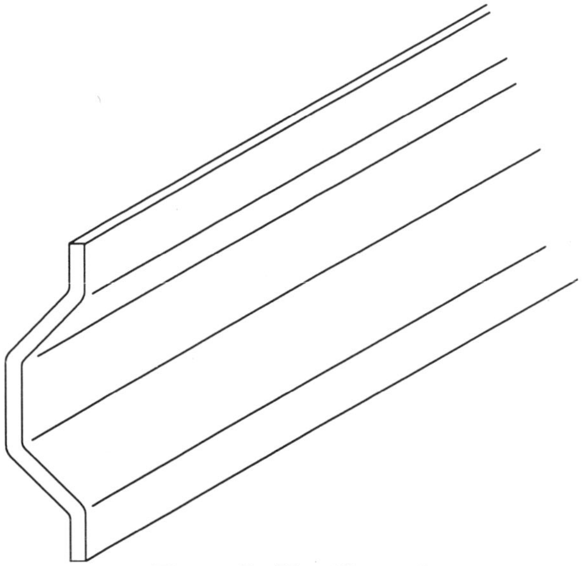

Figure 7. Hat Channel

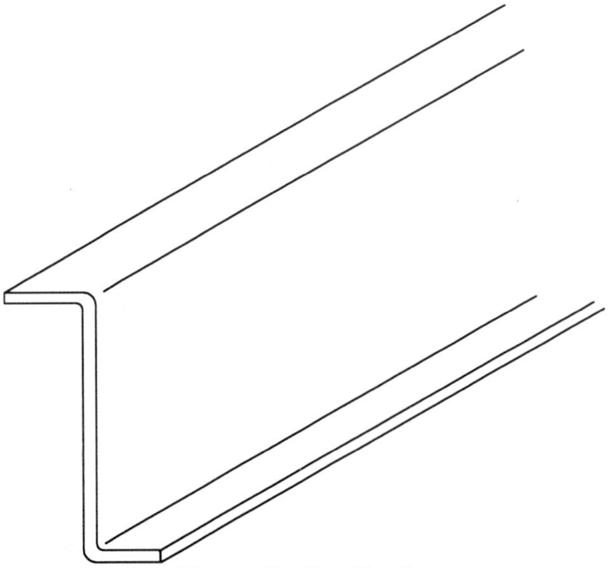

Figure 8. Zee Purlin

DOUBLE BEAM

NESTED BEAM

Figure 9. Built-Up Beams

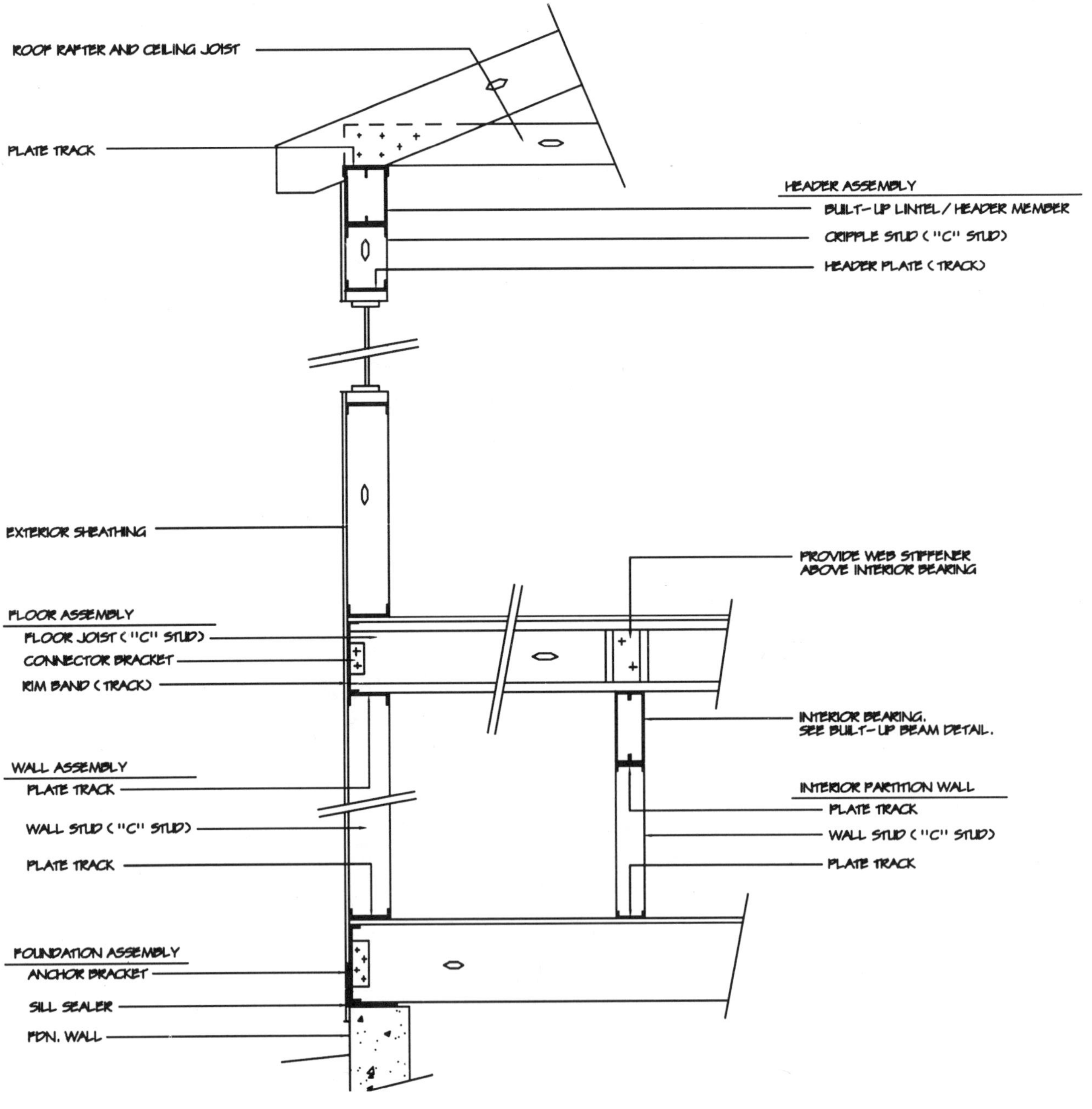

Figure 10. Steel-Framing Wall Section

Cost Estimate

Based on information from various steel framing manufacturers, installed costs range from $7.25 to $10.00 per square foot of floor area. These figures apply to framing for walls (both exterior and interior), floors, and roofs; sheathing and insulation are not included in this estimate. Factors affecting price include the complexity of the floor plan and roof line, type of construction (stick-built or prefabricated), and local labor rates.

INFORMATION SOURCE

Additional information on steel framing can be obtained from:

American Iron and Steel Institute
1101 17th Street, NW, Suite 1300
Washington, DC 20036
(202) 452-7100

Foam Core Structural Sandwich Panels

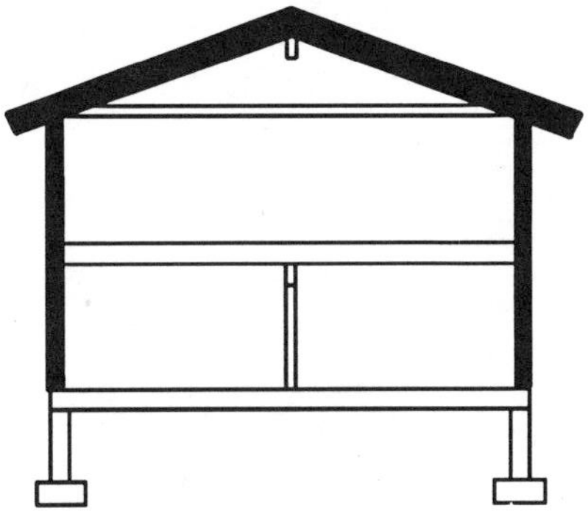

Foam core structural panels are structural members made of two strong, stiff skins—typically OSB or plywood—separated by a light-weight but relatively thick low-density core of expanded polystyrene, extruded polystyrene, or rigid polyurethane.

The U.S. Forest Products Laboratory first began building with structural panels in the 1930s. At that time, most of the panels consisted of plywood skins glued to a core of wood-framing members or paper honeycomb. By today's definition, the panels would have been termed stressed-skin panels. The panels performed in the same way as the more recently developed structural sandwich panels. However, not all stressed-skin panels are necessarily insulated and, conversely, not all foam panels with facings are stressed-skinned.[1] As a result, not all panels are technically alike, although the current literature uses the terms stressed-skin and structural sandwich panels interchangeably. This discussion focuses on structural foam core panels and avoids the term stressed-skin.

The use of structural sandwich panels expanded in the 1950s with the advent of metal-clad refrigerated buildings, which took advantage of the panels' superior energy performance. Today, however, the structural foam core industry is relatively small. A recent study by the Natural Resources Research Institute estimates that 3,750 structural foam core structures were built in 1990. This total represents less than 1 percent of all U.S. single-family homes built in 1990.[2]

Advantages

- **Thermal performance.** A major advantage of foam core panel systems is their enhanced energy efficiency. Typical R-values claimed for standard wall panels range

---

[1]Steve Andrews, *Foam-Core Panels and Building Systems: Principles and Practice Plus Product Directory,* Cutter Information Corporation, Arlington, MA 1988, p. 6.

[2]T. Michael Toole and Timothy D. Tonyan, "The Adoption of Innovation Building Systems: A Case Study," *Building Research Journal,* January 1992, p. 22.

from R-23 to R-40. Roof panels generally have even higher R-values owing to their additional thickness. Comparable R-values per inch of insulation are as follows:

fiberglass batts	R-3 to R-3.86
expanded polystyrene	R-4
extruded polystyrene	R-5
urethane or polyisocyanurate	R-6 to R-8

A 4-3/4-inch wide foam core structural sandwich panel sample.

In addition, since most panels incorporate little solid framing, panel systems are gap-free; therefore, heat loss through thermal bridging is significantly reduced.

- **Speed of construction.** The use of structural foam core panel construction typically reduces the time required to dry-in a home. With the use of large panels, manufacturers claim that houses can be enclosed and ready for windows in a few days.

- **Strength.** When subjected to loading, a structural panel performs much like an I-beam. The skins act as flanges and resist tension and compression, while the core acts as a web, resisting shear and preventing the wrinkling of the skins. Depending on the manufacturer and application, framing members may or may not be integral to the panels themselves. Some building officials are skeptical of such a studless structure. However, when tested to failure, panels usually exceed minimum standards by large margins. Despite the inherent strength of the panels, builders must take care that the manufacturer selected to supply the panels has instituted a structural testing program and that the panels are acceptable under local building codes.

- **Moisture migration.** Because the insulating materials used in the panel's core have inherent vapor-retarding characteristics, an additional vapor barrier is not typically required. In fact, depending on the thickness and density of the core, most urethanes and some polystyrenes have a permeability rating of less than 1, which technically qualifies the panel as a vapor barrier.

Disadvantages

- **Interfacing with other trades.** Foam panels pose a learning curve for certain tradepersons, particularly carpenters, electricians, and plumbers. (These issues are addressed in detail in the discussion on installation.) Manufacturer participation in the early phases of design can eliminate many problems associated with the installation of mechanical systems.

- **Insects.** Much like conventional framing members, foam core panels are susceptible to carpenter ant and termite infestations. Even though there is less wood to be eaten, tunneling in the foam can reduce insulation values and structural integrity. In addition to suggesting standard preventive practice, some manufacturers incorporate insect repellent treatments into the manufacturing process.

- **Roof shingles overheating.** Because of concern over roof shingle overheating, some manufacturers of asphalt shingles do not provide a full-term guarantee on shingles installed over structural sandwich panels. In general, panel manufacturers dispute claims of overheating, yet several now offer roof panels with a built-in air flow channel to ensure shingle durability.

Installation

This description of typical panel installation highlights several important construction process challenges. Perhaps the most important challenge concerns the relationship among the panel manufacturer, the builder, and the home owner, all of whom should come to agreement on house design and details earlier and in more detail than in the case of conventional construction. The design data then can be used to support the automated manufacture of the panel system to a specified design.

Installation of foam core wall panels.

- **Assembly.** Typically, wall panels are 3½, 5½, or 7¼ inches thick while roof panels are either 9¼ or 11¼ inches thick to accommodate conventional framing members. Not all panel systems are manufactured or installed in the same way; there is no standard panel construction technique. Some manufacturers offer installation training for builders and crews interested in learning the technique; others provide their own crews.

  Panel erection requires some tools and equipment not normally used in conventional construction. For roof panels and larger wall panels, a small (12-ton) crane is recommended for placement and installation. Some type of winch-and-strap system is often helpful to ensure that panel edges are butted tight against each other. A router and special bits may be required to cut openings in panels. An extra-large circular saw is sometimes used for cuts not perpendicular to the faces, such as at the roof ridge or eave.

Placement of the wall panels starts by routing out the foam core at the bottom of the panel to allow both panel facings to slip down over the bottom plate. The second panel is set over the bottom plate in the same manner and slid into place next to the first. Connecting splines are then inserted, caulked, and fastened (as discussed in the section on connecting splines). The remaining wall panels are placed in similar fashion. Rough openings for doors and windows can be cut on site with a circular saw or chain saw, although some manufacturers provide panels with completely pre-cut door and window openings. Foam around the perimeter of rough openings is typically routed back to a depth of 1½ inches to let in 2x4 framing. Structural headers are installed as required.

Foam panel construction is compatible with either a platform-frame (as described above) or balloon-frame system (Figure 11). With balloon framing, the lower-floor wall panel bears directly on the sill plate, and the second-level floor framing hangs from the top plate of the lower-floor wall panels. This method offers better thermal performance by keeping the insulation intact. Roof panel installation is similar to that for wall panels, with the same joint conditions. If the roof panels have deep enough sections and load conditions allow, panels can span the distance from the ridge beam to the exterior walls. Typically, floor and roof panels span up to 12 feet.

Conventional framing methods can be substituted or incorporated for some building components. Floors and interior walls, for example, can be framed with conventional joists, especially where they do not need to be insulated. Stick framing also can be used in complicated situations such as bay windows.

- **Connecting splines.** While there are several methods of joining adjacent panels, the splines shown in Figure 12 are the most common. The single 2x spline is simple but results in a thermal bridge. The double spline requires more time for installation but offers better thermal performance. Regardless of which splining method is used, all joints should be properly sealed. Sealants or adhesives should be used at the top and bottom plates as well as between adjacent panels. Using large panels means fewer joints to seal. Since OSB and plywood can expand, the facing should be left a little short where two panels meet at a joint.

- **Electrical and plumbing.** Most manufacturers offer their panels with a built-in chase for wiring. Typically, the chase runs horizontally along the entire width of the panel at about 14 inches above the floor. Vertical channels can be added where required by drilling through the top or bottom plate and reaming a hole through the foam with a piece of metal pipe or conduit. Larger chases for plumbing lines can be precut at the factory.

  Panel manufacturers should be involved in designing the wiring and plumbing plan. Most problems can be avoided with good planning. Some situations call for wiring to be threaded through the chase as panels are installed; in other situations, wiring can be snaked through the chase after the wall is in place. A baseboard raceway is another wiring alternative.

Cost Estimate

Based on information from various manufacturers, to frame a house using foam core panels for the exterior walls and roof and dimension lumber for floors and partitions costs from $8.75 to $11.00 per square foot of panel area. Typically, foam core panel packages include exterior wall and roof systems only (which provide framing, sheathing, and insulation). Factors affecting price include the complexity of the floor plan and the roof line, and local labor rates.

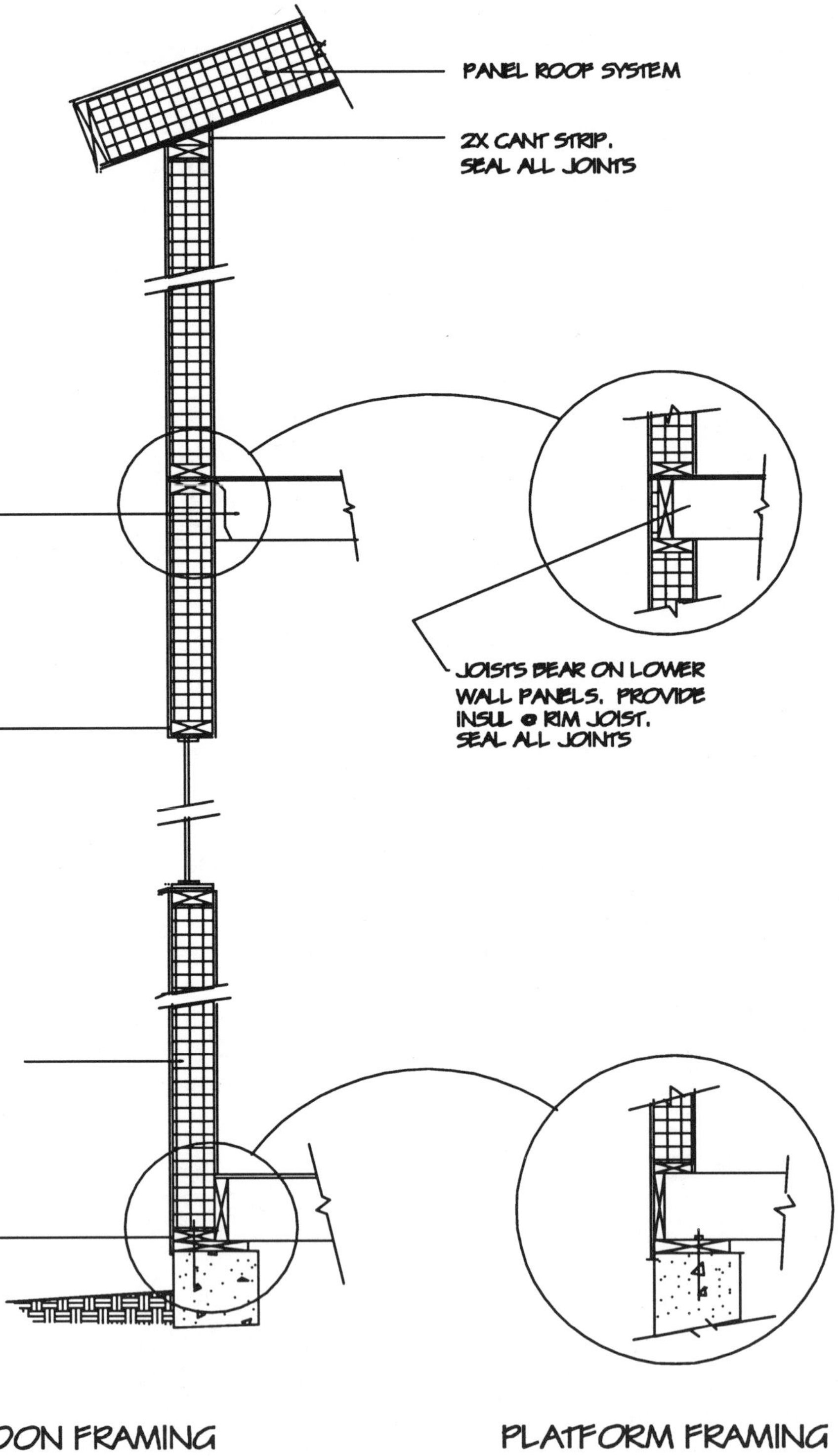

Figure 11. Foam Core Panel Wall Section

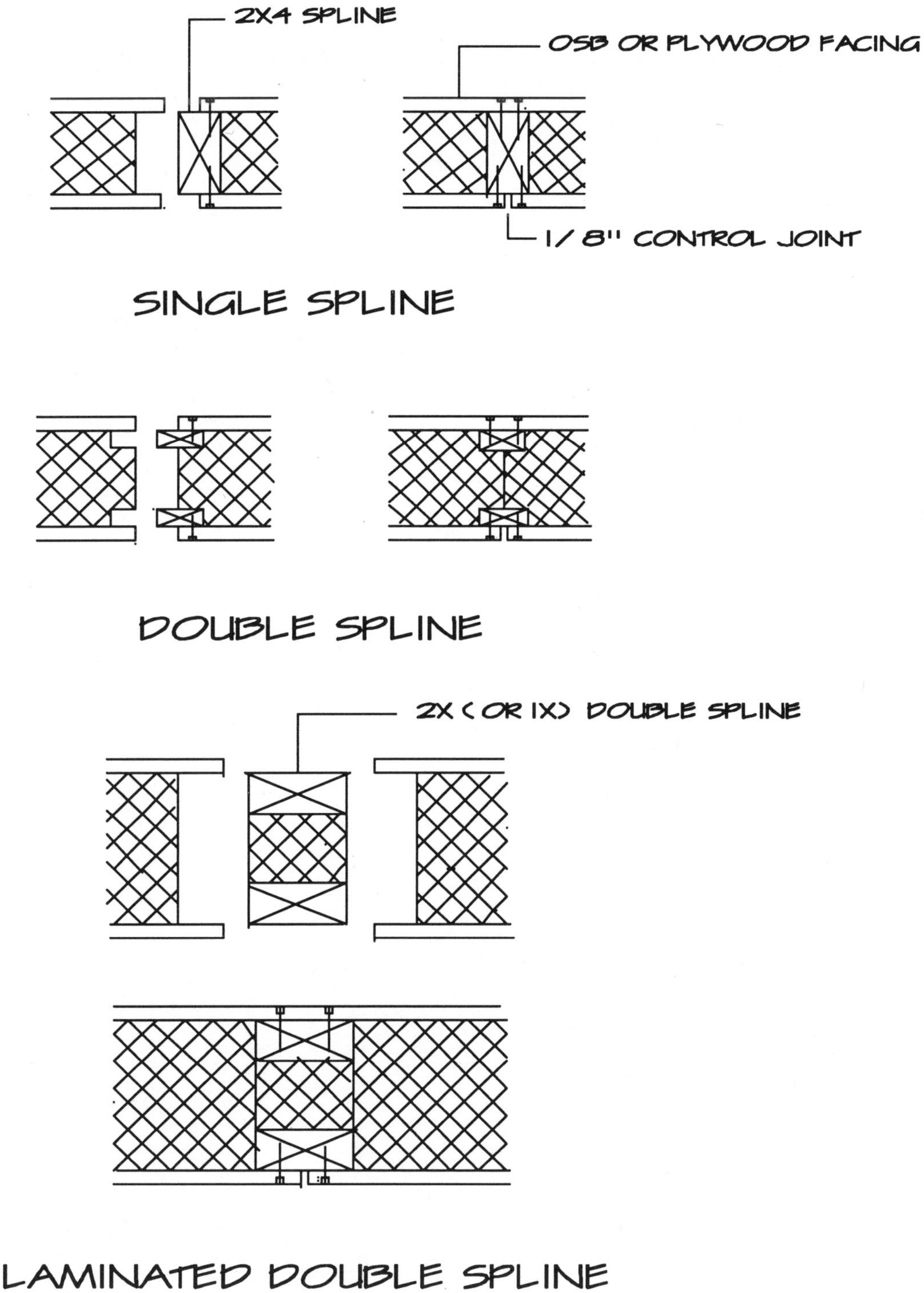

Figure 12. Foam Core Panel Connecting Splines
(Source: *Journal of Light Construction*, February 1992, p. 14)

INFORMATION SOURCE

Additional information on foam core structural sandwich panels can be obtained from:

Building Systems Councils
National Association of Home Builders
1201 15th Street, NW
Washington, DC 20005
(202) 822-0576

Concrete Wall Systems

In the past, the above-grade use of concrete in residential construction has been limited to moderate climates because of concrete's relatively low insulative properties. However, with the development of insulated systems, concrete now offers new opportunities for residential construction. While the concept of combining insulating and structural materials is not new, it is only in the last 10 years that the use of combined systems has started to expand. Because several systems are now available, this discussion compares only the features that make certain types of systems unique and examines the products of several manufacturers as examples. The various systems can be used alone or in different combinations.

The advantages and disadvantages of each system are discussed in the appropriate sections. The thermal performance of insulated concrete wall systems is, however, addressed collectively.

When considering options for insulating concrete or masonry walls, it is important to keep the concepts of superinsulation and thermal lag in proper perspective. Superinsulation traditionally emphasizes the reduced transmission of heat through the building envelope by increasing R-values to achieve better thermal performance. R-values, however, can give an incomplete measure of a building's thermal performance by failing to account for variations in temperature and the thermal storage capacity of materials.

Structures with high thermal mass are able to delay the transfer of heat due to the heat capacity of the building mass. The thermal mass of a material such as concrete has sufficient heat capacity to store thermal energy during the part of the day when the energy is least needed and to release it later when most needed. This is a definite advantage, but only if the outdoor temperature variations fall in a suitable range. More research is needed to quantify the energy-conserving importance of thermal mass in various climates.

The new developments for insulating masonry walls can reduce conductive heat loss by using insulation and improving heat retention capacity with mass. The result is an insulated concrete wall with an R-value of 20 or more, if desired.

INSULATED CONCRETE WALL FORMS

Used to create foundation and exterior walls in residential and commercial construction, insulated wall forms fall into two basic categories: concrete cast between two rigid polystyrene foam panels and stackable, interlocking blocks of plastic foam insulation whose hollow cores are filled with concrete.

LITE-FORM™

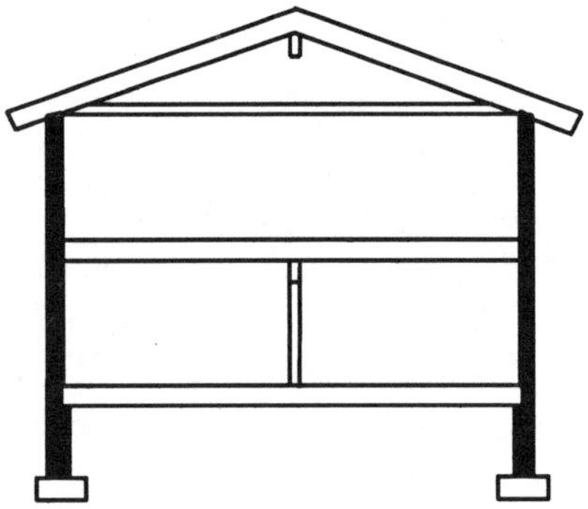

An example of a product in the first category is manufactured by Lite-Form™. Lite-Form™ is an insulated wall form system that uses panels of plastic foam insulation as formwork, separates the panels with plastic ties, and then fills the space between the panels with concrete. The insulation panels remain in place, resulting in a wall insulated on both sides.

Advantages

- **Thermal performance.** The fully insulated wall minimizes thermal breaks and has an R-value of approximately 20.

- **Durability.** Because the insulation remains in place, thermal expansion and contraction of the wall is decreased, thereby reducing cracking.

- **Speed of construction.** Skilled labor is not required for installation, and the forms' light weight permits either on-site assembly by a single worker or factory fabrication in sections for transport to the job site. The forms are left in place, thereby eliminating costly stripping; drywall can be screwed directly into the form ties, thereby eliminating the need for furring strips.

- **Extends construction season.** The insulation permits concrete to be cast in cold weather.

Disadvantage

- **Extra care required during casting.** If the concrete is cast too quickly, the forms can blow out and cause damage and waste. In accordance with the manufacturer's recommendations, a dry slump and pump truck with a hydraulic boom should eliminate this problem. Extra care must also be taken during backfill to avoid damage to the foam panels.

Installation

Form sections are built by assembling 8-foot-long x 8-inch-high polystyrene panels with special form ties and corner ties (Figure 13). The wall form is built course by course, stacking the

Lite-Form™ concrete wall forming system being placed before pour.

standard 8-inch panels to the desired height. The form is placed on a footing or directly on the ground if the soil bearing capacity is adequate. It is then braced, reinforced, and filled with concrete. Exterior siding or interior drywall can be screwed into the plastic ties. The polystyrene that is above grade and remains exposed after the exterior siding is installed, should be covered with a trowel-applied protective coating. Electrical and plumbing lines can be installed within the 2-inch thickness of the polystyrene, although some local codes may require conduit.

Cost Estimate

Based on a synthesis of manufacturer claims and Research Center estimates, installed costs range from \$4.50 to \$6.50 per square foot of wall area. Lite-Form™ is typically an insulated exterior wall system only; roof and floor systems are not reflected in this price. Factors affecting price include the complexity of the floor plan and local labor rates.

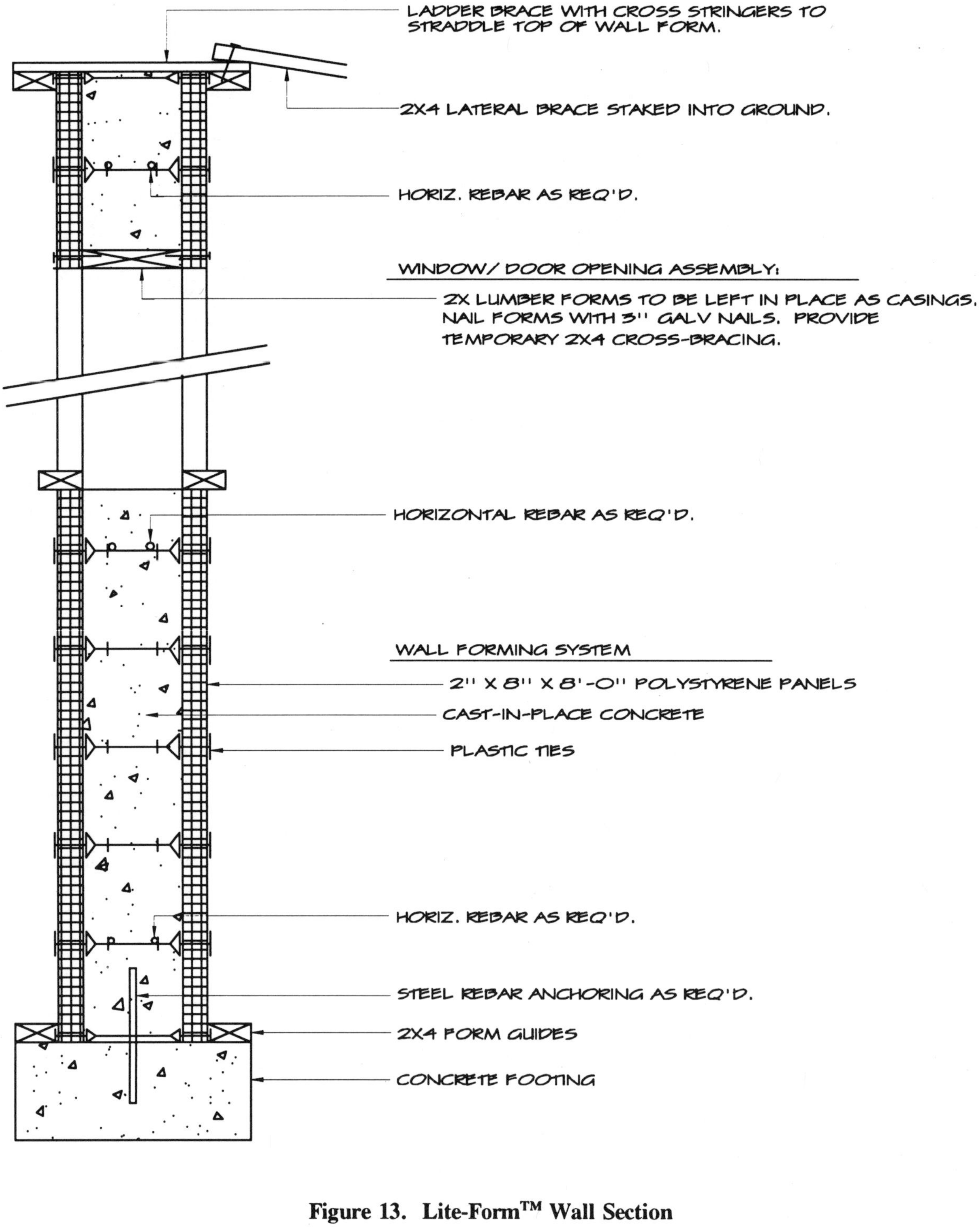

Figure 13. Lite-Form™ Wall Section

ENER-G-BLOCK™

A product manufactured by Creston Technologies is representative of the second type of insulated wall form system. Ener-G-Block™ involves the stacking of hollow blocks of cellular polyurethane (Figure 14), which are then filled with concrete to create insulated concrete walls.

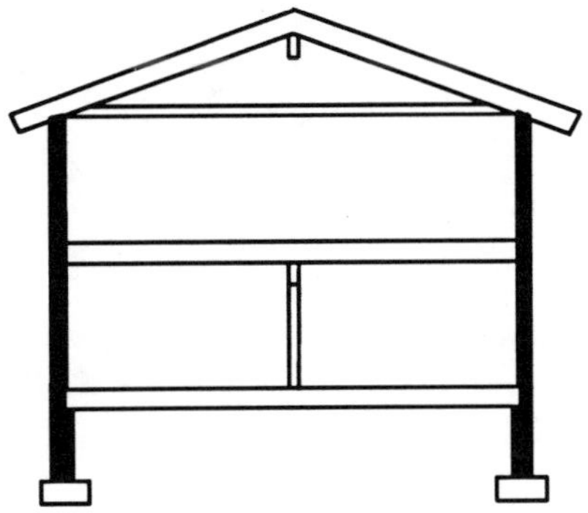

Advantages

Many of the advantages listed above for Lite-Form™, namely, thermal performance, speed of construction, and durability, apply to Ener-G-Block™ as well.

Installation

Creston's Ener-G-Blocks™ are 8 inches x 8 inches x 16 inches and weigh only 14 ounces. The blocks are stacked course by course and joined together with an interlocking tongue and groove. Stacking the blocks is very easy, so unskilled labor can be used. The blocks' hollow cores are stacked over vertical reinforcing rods placed according to local code. Once the block wall has reached the required height and adequate bracing is provided, concrete is cast into the blocks. Furring may be required for some exterior and interior finish materials. Electrical and plumbing lines can be installed within the thickness of the polyurethane block.

Cost Estimate

The manufacturer claims that installed costs range from $5.25 to $5.75 per square foot of wall area. Depending on the region of the country, additional shipping costs could be added. Ener-G-Block™ is an insulated exterior wall system only; roof and floor systems as well as furring required for finish materials are not reflected in this price. Factors affecting price include the complexity of the floor plan and local labor rates.

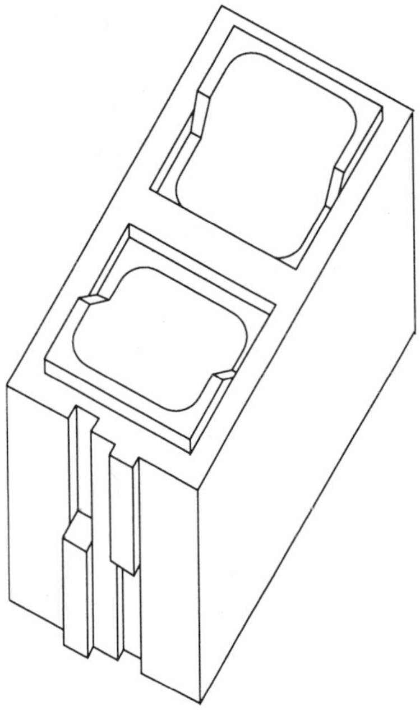

Figure 14. Ener-G-Block™

INSULATED CONCRETE WALL SYSTEMS

Another insulated concrete wall system is manufactured by Composite Technologies under the brand name Thermomass™. This system involves centering a panel of plastic foam insulation between two conventional metal or wood forms. The panel is held in place by proprietary "connectors" (Figure 15). Concrete is then cast into the forms.

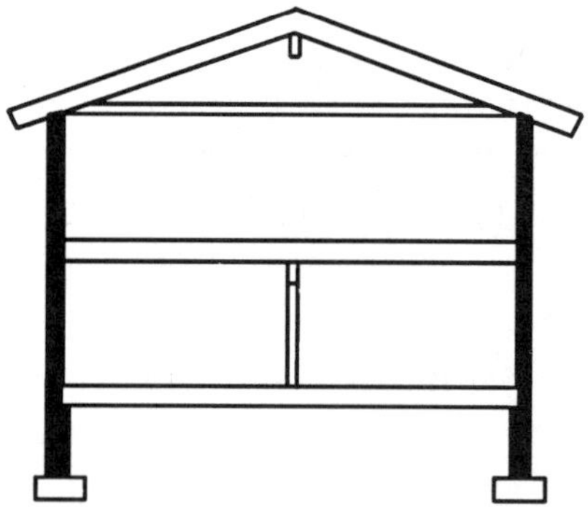

Disadvantage

- **Increased Labor.** The complexity of the system, particularly the use of special connectors, means that the concrete must be cast evenly on both sides of the insulation. Further, the system requires the use of conventional forms, which must be removed, cleaned, and stored.

Installation

The principal element of the Thermomass™ system is its proprietary connectors, which are 10 or 12 inches long and fabricated of pultruded fiber-reinforced vinyl with molded plastic collars (Figures 15 and 16). The connectors hold a 2- to 4-inch-thick rigid insulation panel in place between two conventional forms. The connectors can be installed by either drilling holes in the panel or using a predrilled panel manufactured specifically for this application. Concrete is then cast directly over the center of the panel so that one-half falls into the space on either side of the board; the forms are later stripped. Furring may be required for exterior and interior finish materials as well as for electrical and plumbing lines. Some utilities can be located in a chase routed in the concrete.

Cost Estimate

The manufacturer claims an installed cost of $5.50 per square foot of wall area. The system is typically an insulated exterior wall component only; roof and floor systems, interior walls, and the furring required for finish materials are not reflected in this price. Factors affecting price include the complexity of the floor plan and local labor rates.

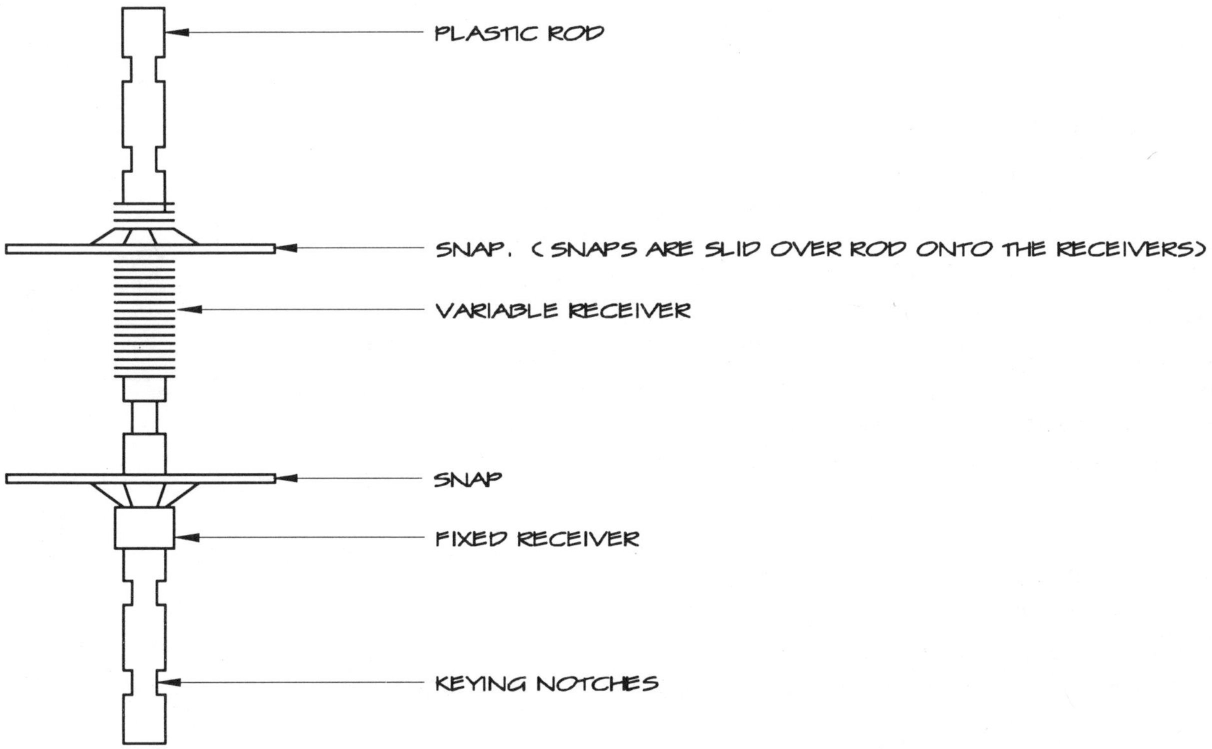

Figure 15. Thermomass™ "Connector"
(Source: Product Literature)

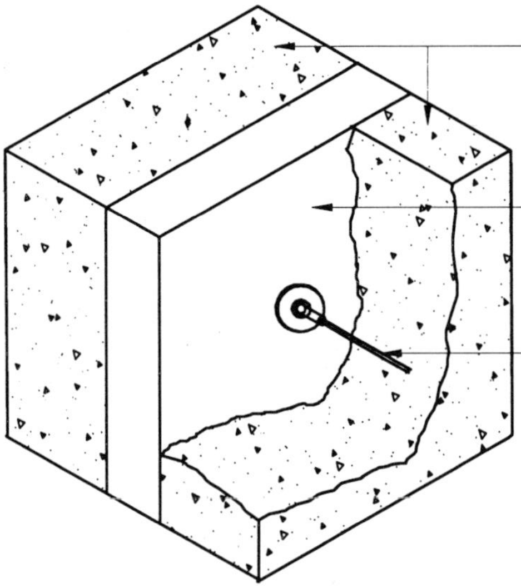

Figure 16. Wall Profile of Thermomass™ System
(Source: Product Literature)

WELDED-WIRE SANDWICH PANELS

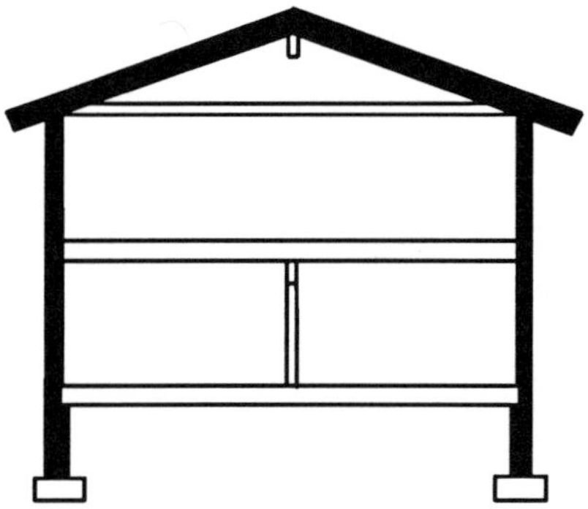

Welded-wire sandwich panels provide the framework and structural reinforcement for a panel construction system. They consist of a three-dimensional welded-wire space frame integrated with a foam plastic insulation core, which varies in thickness. The panels are completed at the site with a layer of shotcrete, although the exterior layer may be precast. The panels can be used as floors, load-bearing walls, partition walls, or roofs.

Insteel Construction Systems, Inc., the leading manufacturer of welded-wire panels, has received a National Evaluation Report from CABO. For more information regarding loading, fire resistance ratings, and other technical data related to design, refer to CABO Report No. NER-454.

A welded-wire sandwich panel sample with 2½-inch rigid insulation core.

Advantages

- **Speed of construction.** Welded-wire sandwich panels typically reduce the time to dry-in a home. The light-weight panels (a standard panel weighs 1.2 pounds per square foot) are easy to handle; heavy equipment is not required. With the use of large panels, manufacturers claim that houses can be enclosed and ready for windows in a few days.

- **Fire rating.** The panels' finished surface is concrete, which offers up to a two-hour fire rating (valid for fire exposure from either side).

- **Durability.** The shotcrete produces a monolithic structure resistant to high winds, moisture, and termites.

Disadvantage

Most local codes require structural calculations by a registered professional.

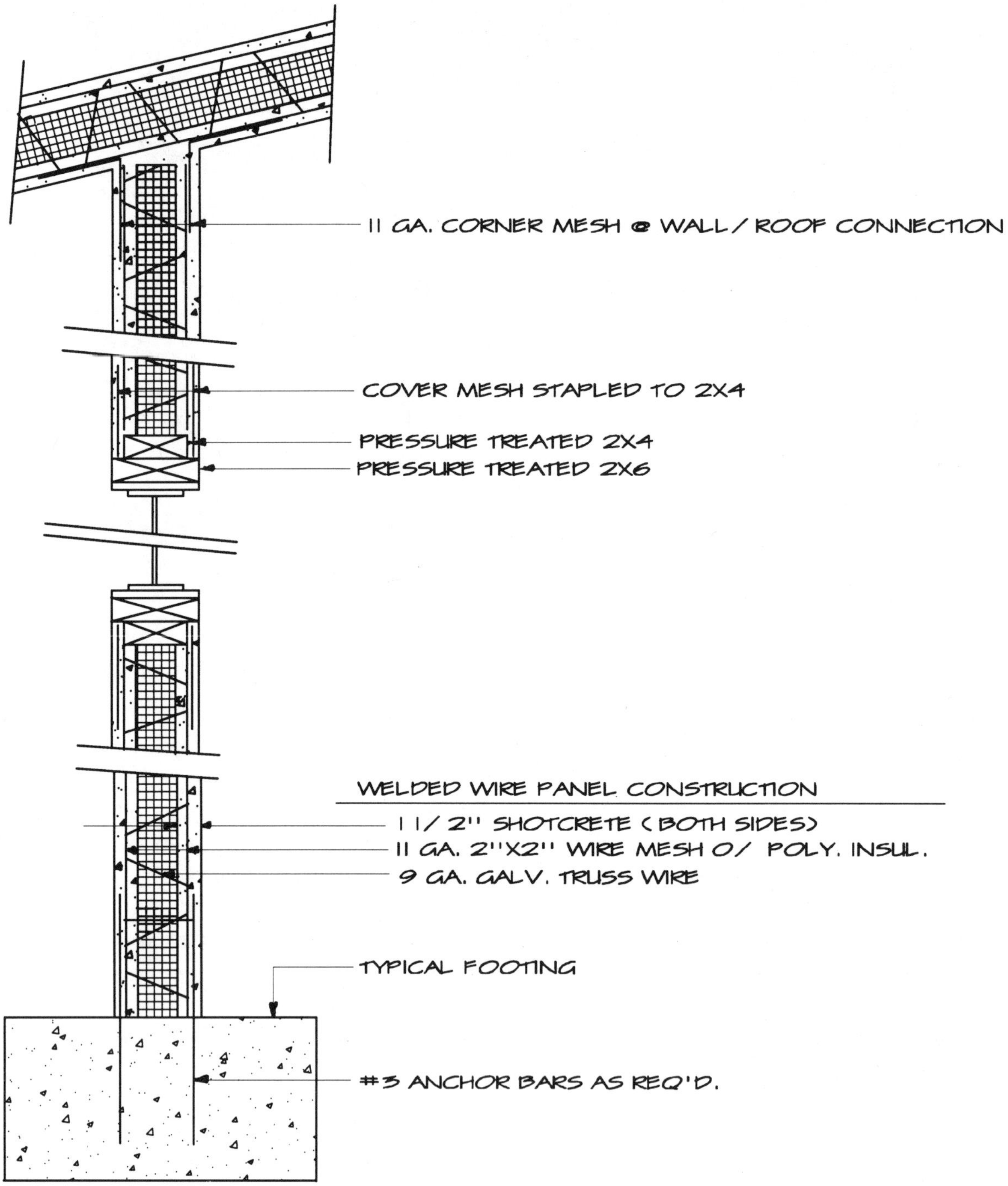

Figure 17. Welded-Wire Sandwich Panel Wall Section
(Source: Compilation of details provided by manufacturer)

Installation

A standard panel is 4 feet long x 8 feet wide x 5½ inches thick, including the finish coat of shotcrete. Panels are available in lengths up to 24 feet. The panels are erected and spliced together by using lap mesh, rebar, and tie wire. Cutouts for openings can be made at the job site or at the factory by using bolt cutters or a reciprocating saw for windows and doors. Electrical and plumbing lines are inserted within the panel between the wire and the foam. Once assembled, the panels are completed with a 1- to 1½-inch layer of shotcrete on each side and hand trowelled for the desired finish (Figure 17). Depending on the desired finish, furring may be required for interior drywall.

Cost Estimate

The manufacturer claims that installed costs range from $5.00 to $5.75 per square foot of panel area. The panels typically provide an insulated exterior wall and roof system only; the floor system, interior walls, and any furring required for finish materials are not reflected in this price. Factors affecting price include the complexity of the floor plan and the roof line, and local labor rates.

INFORMATION SOURCES

Additional information on concrete wall systems can be obtained from:

National Concrete Masonry Association
2302 Horse Pen Road
Herndon, VA 22071
(703) 713-3406

National Ready Mixed Concrete Association
900 Spring Street
Silver Spring, MD 20910
(301) 587-1400

Portland Cement Association
5420 Old Orchard Road
Skokie, IL 60077-1093
(708) 966-6200

Concrete Block Construction

Concrete masonry units (CMU) have long been a widely used alternative to wood and, in many moderate climates such as Florida, concrete block construction is common in residential construction. The material's ready availability and low labor costs for installation make concrete block a viable option for areas that do not require materials with high insulating properties.

Traditional concrete blocks are composed of portland cement, a fine aggregate and water. The standard blocks (including the ⅜-inch thick mortar head and bed joints) are 8-inches high and 16-inches long. CMUs, however, vary in size, weight, texture, strength and coeffecients of heat transmission based on the type of aggregate used. Using shale, clay or slag as an aggregate, for example, decreases the weight and increases the insulating value compared to sand or gravel.

The primary advantage of CMU construction is the building industry's familiarity with the technique. Most builders, engineers, and architects are familiar with the process, and all the model building codes recognize concrete block construction. Additionally, concrete masonry has proven to be a durable material for hundreds of years and is not expensive to maintain.

The thermal performance of standard block, however, is such that when used in areas other than moderate climates, additional insulation is usually required. This is typically accomplished either with insulation placed between furring strips fastened to the interior face of the wall or with the insulation applied as a substrate for an exterior finish such as stucco. When deep furring strips are used, plumbing and electrical lines can be installed in the wall cavity along with the insulation.

The concrete block construction technique is well documented. Several new types of block are being developed by various manufacturers, and some are discussed in the following sections.

INSULATED CONCRETE BLOCK SYSTEMS

New insulating techniques have been incorporated into concrete block construction. Although different manufacturers have developed a wide variety of systems, this section focuses on a few representative examples. Generally, blocks are insulated by placing a fill material in the blocks as the wall is built or by placing plastic inserts into the cores of conventional block or using blocks with specially designed cores.

Insulated block systems offer superior durability and fire resistance because the insulation is located inside rather than outside the wall. Advantages and disadvantages specific to each product are discussed in the respective product sections.

INTEGRA™

One type of concrete block system uses fill materials such as loose beads of expanded polystyrene, loose vermiculite, or foamed-in-place insulation. An example of this type of system is Integra™, developed by Superlite Builders Supply, Inc. This system involves laying a block wall and filling the core with foam. Poured into the cores as a liquid, the foam then expands to fill the voids.

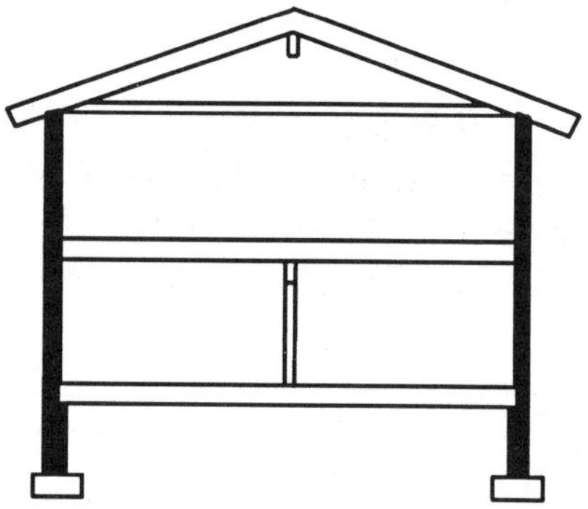

Disadvantage

Superlite provides structural engineering for a building but, depending on the building size, may charge an additional fee. Further, Superlite Builders or its appointed licensee must post tension the walls and install the polyurethane insulation.

Installation

The Integra™ system involves laying grade N-type I open-end concrete masonry units in running bond with type S mortar. The wall is laid with horizontal joint reinforcing and with vertical steel tension rods used for post tensioning to strengthen the wall and to resist uplift loads (Figure 18). A proprietary blended polyurethane is then poured into the block cavities. The wall is capped with a wood plate that is part of the post tensioning system. Furring may be required for certain finish materials as well as for electrical and plumbing lines. Some utilities can be located in a chase routed in the concrete.

Cost Estimate

The manufacturer claims an installed cost of $3.70 per square foot of wall area. Typically, the system provides an insulated exterior wall only; floor and roof systems, interior walls, and furring required for finish materials are not reflected in this price. Factors affecting price include the complexity of the floor plan and local labor rates.

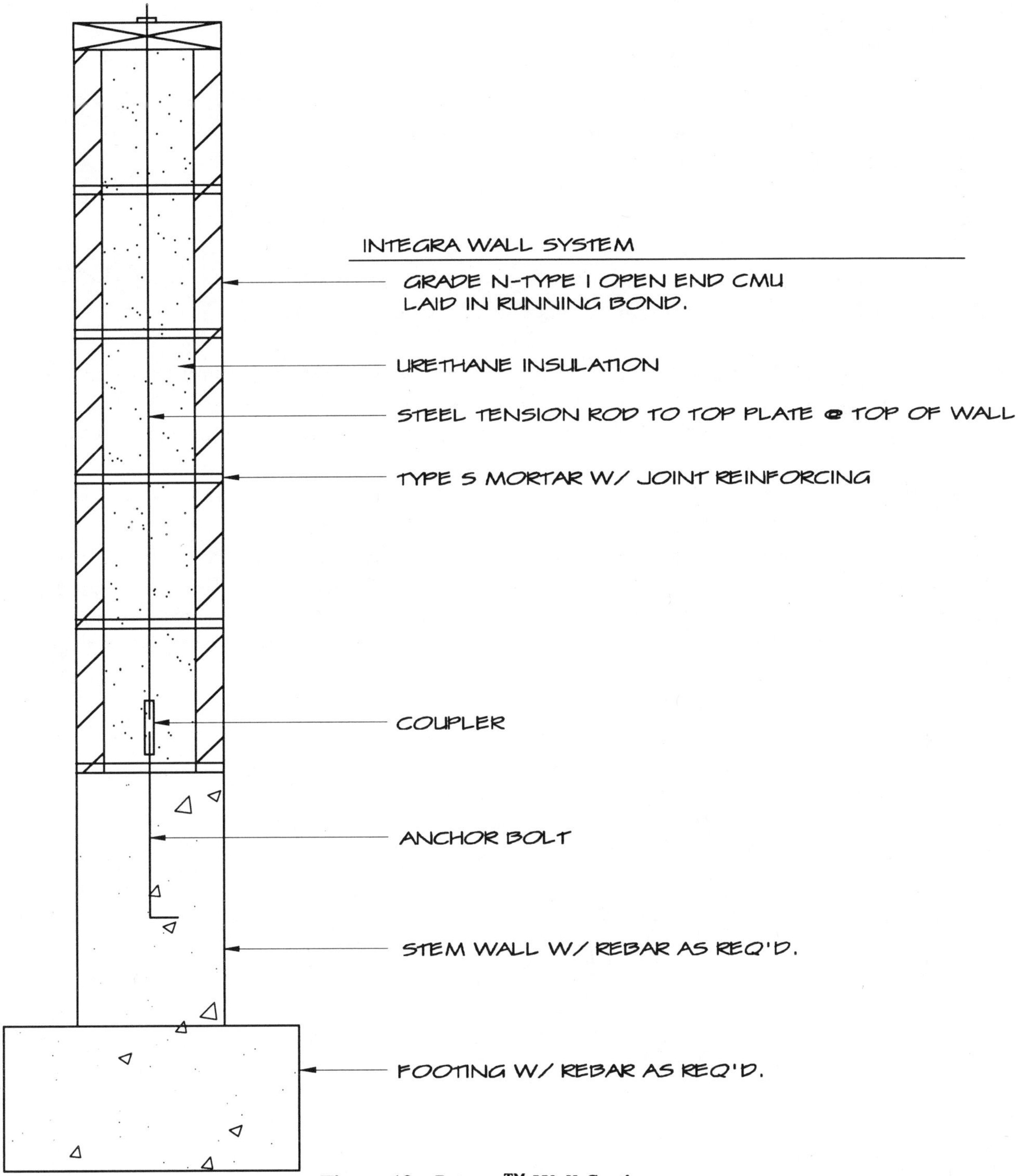

Figure 18. Integra™ Wall Section
(Source: Product Literature)

THERMA-LOCK™

A second type of insulating concrete block uses plastic inserts that are usually installed in the manufacturing plant. The Therma-Lock™ system developed by Therma-Lock Products, Inc., is an example (Figure 19).

Advantages

- **Speed of construction.** Because the blocks arrive on site already insulated and ready to be laid, no additional labor is required to insulate the wall.

- **Thermal performance.** Because no concrete webs extend through the block, thermal bridging through the block is eliminated. In addition, the manufacturer claims that the design eliminates thermal bridging through both the vertical and horizontal mortar joints.

Installation

Even though the Therma-Lock™ block design is unique, the blocks are stacked with mortar in the same manner as conventional block. The blocks are available in 8-, 10-, and 12-inch depths. The manufacturer claims respective R-values of 15, 19, and 24. Furring may be required for certain finish materials as well as for electrical and plumbing lines. Some utilities can be located in a chase routed in the concrete.

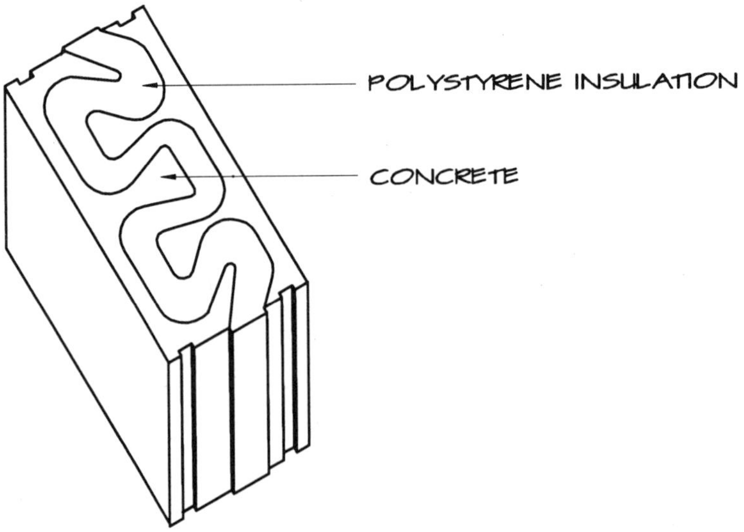

Figure 19. Therma-Lock™ Insulated Concrete Block

Cost Estimate

The manufacturer claims that installed costs range from $5.75 to $6.25 per square foot of wall area. Typically, Therma-Lock™ provides an insulated exterior wall system only; floor and roof systems, interior walls, and furring required for finish materials are not reflected in this price. Factors affecting price include the complexity of the floor plan and local labor rates.

SPARFIL (STRUCTURAL LIGHT-WEIGHT CONCRETE)

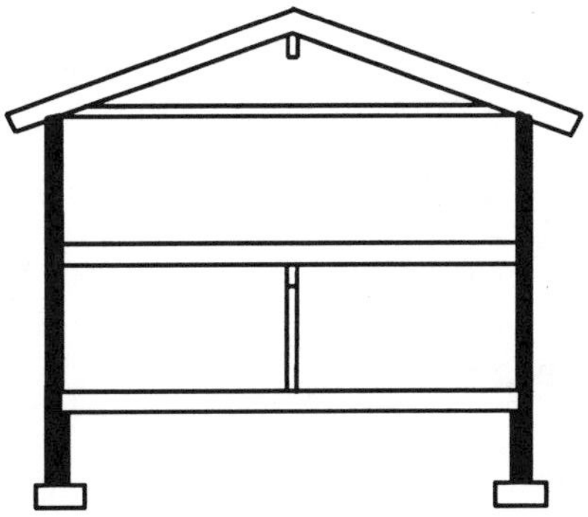

Another approach to insulating concrete is to change the properties of the concrete itself. Currently, research and development of cement-based materials is experiencing a rebirth. Admixtures and light-weight aggregates are making concrete stronger, lighter, and more workable. Aggregates most commonly used for structural light-weight concrete include expanded shales, clays, and slates; sintered shales and clays; pelletized or extruded fly ash; and expanded slags. The raw materials are heated to entrap gas or steam in the softened material, which, in turn, forms a cellular structure lighter in weight than the sand or gravel used in conventional concrete.[1] Blending insulating materials such as light-weight aggregates or plastic foam insulation beads also decreases the density of the concrete, thereby increasing its insulative value.

While many different light-weight concretes are undergoing development, few are commercially available today.

SPARFIL concrete is a mixture of Portland cement, sand, expanded polystyrene beads, a proprietary additive, and water. The polystyrene beads constitute 60 to 65 percent of the product by volume. The manufacturer claims that an 8-inch concrete block has an R-value of 8. When fitted with inserts, the same block has an increased R-value of 13 (Figure 20). The manufacturer claims that a 12-inch block with inserts has an R-value of 25.

---

[1]Martha G. VanGeem, *The Construction Specifier,* Construction Technology Laboratories, Inc., Skokie, IL, December 1989.

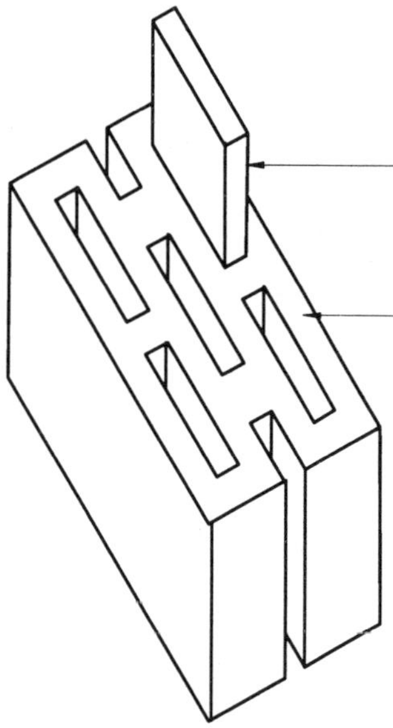

Figure 20. SPARFIL Light-Weight Concrete Block with Inserts

Advantage

The light-weight blocks (27 pounds versus about 35 pounds for a standard block) are drystacked and surface bonded. The result is reduced labor costs and very low air infiltration rates. The surface bonding also provides a good moisture barrier.

Installation

The SPARFIL blocks are drystacked after the first course. Both sides of the block are coated with a surface bonding cement that structurally joins the blocks together. In situations where additional vertical reinforcement is required (such as areas with high seismic activity, a high water table, or high winds) the manufacturer recommends using the 12-inch block, which has voids large enough to accommodate steel rebar and a grout fill. A finished coat may be applied over the bonding coat. Furring may be required for certain finish materials as well as for electrical and plumbing lines.

Cost Estimate

The manufacturer claims that installed costs range from $8.00 to $12.00 per square foot of wall area. Typically, SPARFIL blocks provide an insulated exterior wall system only; floor and roof systems, interior walls, and furring required for finish materials are not reflected in this price. Factors affecting price include the complexity of the floor plan and local labor rates.

INFORMATION SOURCES

Additional information on concrete block construction can be obtained from:

National Concrete Masonry Association
2302 Horse Pen Road
Herndon, VA 22071
(703) 713-3406

National Precast Concrete Association
825 East 64th Street
Indianapolis, IN 46220
(317) 571-9500

National Ready Mixed Concrete Association
900 Spring Street
Silver Spring, MD 20910
(301) 587-1400

Portland Cement Association
5420 Old Orchard Road
Skokie, IL 60077-1083
(708) 966-6200

Emerging Technologies

Table 7 lists technologies currently under development that are expected to be commercially available in the United States within the next five years.

Table 7
Alternatives to Lumber and Plywood
(emerging technologies)

Alternative	Definition	Building Component
Autoclaved Cellular Concrete	Precast, structural light-weight concrete blocks and panels	Wall systems, roofing materials
Arrowood™	Laminated composition of LVL flanges and a solid 1½-inch OSB web	Headers, joists, and rafters
Timberstrand™	Flakes and short strands of wood fiber adhered under pressure	Currently used as core stock for doors and windows; targeted use as short-span beam and headers
Scrimber™	Small-diameter, debarked logs crushed into woven mats that are stacked, glued, and pressed	Headers, joists, and rafters
WISA-Wood™	Composite wood plank of small-diameter, solid logs	Doors, stair components
Gridcore™	Light-weight structural panel made from recycled wood, paper, and some plastics	Targeted use as wall, floor, and roof systems
Honeycomb Panels	Light-weight panels made from paper and bonded between thin rigid skins of various materials	Interior partition walls
Pultruded Plastic	Composition of fiberglass, graphite, or carbon and resins cured into a high-strength synthetic polymer	Beams, panels, and rebar

AUTOCLAVED CELLULAR CONCRETE

Autoclaved cellular concrete (ACC) is a precast, structural light-weight concrete that can be used for building blocks and panels. ACC is not yet produced in the United States or Canada but is a standard building material in many other countries. However, with funding from the Electric Power Research Institute and participating utility companies, North American Cellular Concrete is building a prototype mobile manufacturing plant to demonstrate the product's potential. After several months in Massachusetts, the mobile plant will be moved to other locations around the country. Because 30 to 40 percent of the block is typically fly ash, which is the byproduct of coal-fired power plants, utility companies are expected to support development of the product.

In addition to fly ash, ACC blocks are produced from cement, lime, water, and a small amount of aluminum. The aluminum causes a chemical reaction that expands the slurry enough to allow the concrete to be stripped from its mold, cut into the required size, and steam-cured in an autoclave. The resulting blocks are light-weight, more thermally efficient than conventional concrete block, fire-resistant, durable, and load-bearing. The blocks can also be cut, routed, sawn, and nailed with conventional carpentry tools. For more information, contact North American Cellular Concrete, Post Office Box 601, Chantilly, VA 22021.

ARROWOOD™

A composite lumber product, Arrowood™ is derived from a combination of the LVL and OSB manufacturing processes. It has the same nominal dimensions as 2x lumber but, with its LVL flanges and OSB web, Arrowood's™ performance characteristics are similar to those of an I-beam. The product is available in sizes up to nominal 2x16-inch lumber in lengths up to 36 feet. Arrowood™ has been approved by CABO under NER426 for use as headers, floor joists, and roof rafters. Although the product was previously manufactured by Fibreboard Technologies, it is not currently being produced. Fibreboard Technologies is seeking new investors.

TIMBERSTRAND™

Similar to parallel strand lumber (PSL), Timberstrand™ is produced by gluing together long, narrow strands of dried wood. Timberstrand's components, however, are more "flake"-like than PSL, resulting in a lower-cost product with somewhat limited structural properties. Timberstrand™ currently is not approved for structural use, but is used as core stock for doors and windows. Its manufacturers are targeting the product for use as short-span beams and headers in the near future.

SCRIMBER™

Also similar to PSL, Scrimber™ is manufactured from trees often only 3 to 4 inches in diameter. The trees are debarked and passed through a series of roller mills that crush them into mats of interconnected strands. The strands are then dried, sprayed with glue, and adhered under pressure to their final density. The manufacturers of the product, which was developed in Australia, have not yet sought approval in the United States.

WISA-WOOD™

Manufacturers in Finland are developing a composite wood plank whose component pieces are small-diameter solid logs. The logs, typically between 3 and 8 inches in diameter, are cut into trapezoid-shaped pieces and glued together so that the face pattern is wide-narrow-wide-narrow. The completed planks, which can be made up to 4-feet wide x 10-feet long x up to 3-inches thick, can be used for doors, stair components, and furniture. WISA-Wood™ planks are not yet available in the United States.

GRIDCORE™

A new product manufactured by Noble Franklin Corp., Gridcore™ is a light-weight structural panel made from recycled wood, paper, and some plastics. Still under development, the product does not yet have approval for use as a structural building element. Gridcore™ subpanels are made by placing a fiber slurry into a mold that forms ribs on one side and a flat surface on the other side. Two subpanels are then glued together at the ribbed sides to form a completed panel. The U.S. Department of Agriculture's (USDA) Forest Products Laboratory began development of the product in the early 1970s and dubbed it "spaceboard" in reference to the panels' ribbed core. The USDA licensed Noble Franklin to begin commercialization of the product in June 1992.

HONEYCOMB PANELS

Although honeycomb panel technology was initiated by the U.S. Department of Agriculture in 1944, the product is still in its commercial infancy. Several companies continue to develop the technology, but the product currently does not have code approval for structural applications. The honeycomb panel has a core made of paper impregnated with phenolic resin. The paper is bent into a honeycomb shape and then glued between thin, rigid sheets of various materials such as composite wood panels and gypsum board. A French manufacturer produces a honeycomb panel faced with drywall, providing a one-step procedure for interior partition walls. The company currently does not have any U.S. affiliates.

PLASTICS

In today's age of composite materials, plastic is finding new applications in residential construction. The research and development divisions of the large plastic companies and small inventors are both discovering market niches for new plastic products. Plastic is vaguely defined as the broad range of synthetic polymers made from petroleum and various other chemicals.

The argument surrounding the environmental impact of plastic is paradoxical. Plastic relies largely on a nonrenewable resource—oil—for production, yet many plastics are recyclable and could be used or reused as construction products.

General Electric (GE) has recently completed construction of a $10 million showcase plastic house that displays many potential uses of plastic in residential construction. Although plastic accounts for only 30 percent of the components and the house is, in fact, framed with wood, the GE house illustrates plastic's potential. Examples of plastic-based products include interior wall panels, which, when painted, are similar in appearance to painted drywall; roofing panels, which, as mentioned earlier, are noncombustible; floor tiles that are removable for easier access to electrical or plumbing lines; and fixtures such as one-piece sink units that are easier to install.

Today, few load-bearing applications of plastic exist because pultrusion—the method used to manufacture structural plastic components—is prohibitively expensive. In pultrusion, a composition of fiberglass, graphite, or carbon and resin is cured into a high-strength synthetic polymer. Given their high cost, pultruded products are used in construction where wood or steel would be vulnerable to rot or corrosion or where steel would cause electromagnetic interference. Pultruded plastics, produced in the form of beams, panels, or even rebars have found applications in hospitals, chemical facilities, and radar installations.

At present, plastic is more commonly used in nonstructural applications such as PVC piping, vinyl windows and siding, plastic foam insulation, and moisture barriers. Plastic lumber is also commercially available and, in some cases, uses postconsumer plastic waste as its feedstock. However, postconsumer plastic waste contains several different polymers, all with different properties relating to melt points, strength, and shrinkage. Currently, there are no industry standards for plastic lumber. Nonetheless, plastic lumber does have some functional advantages, namely, weather resistance and fire retardance, both of which make the product well suited to such applications as fences, exterior trim, lawn furniture, and decking material. New plastic roofing systems have found a market in California where some communities have banned combustible roofing materials such as cedar shakes.

When used with other materials, plastic can perform as part of a structural system. Insulated concrete wall forms and structural foam core panels are two such examples that are addressed in other sections of this report. As development continues, plastics will likely offer increasingly innovative design and material options, especially in composition with other materials. A plastic facing applied to wood for both fireproofing and additional strength is one example.

INFORMATION SOURCE

Additional information on plastic can be obtained from:

Society of the Plastics Industry
1275 K Street, NW, Suite 400
Washington, D.C. 20005
(202) 371-5200

Wood-Saving Methods

Under the auspices of the U.S. Department of Housing and Urban Development, the Research Center has produced two manuals on more efficient wood-frame construction. Published in 1971, the *Manual of Lumber and Plywood Saving Techniques* describes methods for reducing lumber and plywood requirements without sacrificing structural integrity. *Reducing Home Building Costs with OVE,* originally released in 1971, has been revised and republished in 1994 as *Cost-Effective Home Building: A Design and Construction Handbook.* Its objective is to reduce construction costs through a systematic approach to building based on efficient design and construction principles, including those that apply to lumber and plywood techniques.

FLOOR AND ROOF FRAMING

Slab-on-Grade Construction

Where site conditions allow, a concrete slab can replace conventional floor framing. The cost effectiveness of slab-on-grade construction has been further enhanced by a building technology called the frost-protected shallow foundation (FPSF), which has been used in Scandinavia for 35 years. The FPSF is based on the principle that heat from a building can be used to prevent the ground under the foundation from freezing and heaving. The technique permits foundations as little as 12 inches deep to be built in very cold climates by the strategic placement of insulation (Figure 21). Although U.S. building codes do not yet recognize the technology, the Research Center is currently working toward code acceptance.

Flat (Parallel Chord) Trusses

Flat trusses are premanufactured trusses composed of LVL or machine stress-rated lumber top and bottom chords. The web/chord connection is made with a metal gusset plate or with various proprietary pin connections. Manufacturers of truss systems publish span tables for their products. Flat trusses can easily span the full depth of a house. Although the depth of the trusses typically exceeds 12 inches, the open web can simplify plumbing and HVAC installation.

24-inch Joist, Truss, or Rafter Spacing

In some cases, the grade or size of joists, trusses, or rafters allows the spacing to be increased from 16 to 24 inches on center. In other cases, the grade or size may have to be increased somewhat. In either case, the result can be labor and material savins. An important complement to 24-inch spacing is glue-nailing the subfloor, thereby creating a structural "T-beam" at each joist. Glued floors can increase joist spans or reduce lumber sizes or grades for a given floor span.

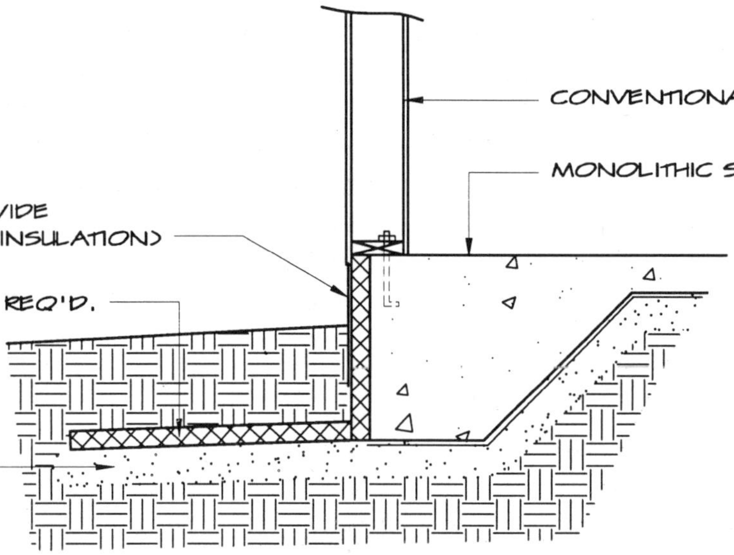

Figure 21. Frost-Protected Shallow Foundation Detail

Elimination of Midspan Bridging

Previous work by the Research Center and the U.S. Forest Products Laboratory has proved that bridging, solid or otherwise, does not add appreciably to floor stiffness or strength. While still required by some local building officials, bridging is no longer required by any of the U.S. model building codes for joists 12 inches or less in depth.

Supporting Nonload-Bearing Partitions

Conventional construction typically calls for double floor joists under nonload-bearing partitions that are parallel to the floor joists. However, where ⅝-inch or ¾-inch plywood flooring is used, no additional support is required, and the partition may be nailed directly to the floor. Partitions parallel to the overhead floor or ceiling joists may be nailed to the 2x blocking (at 24-inch spacing), which serves as a nailer for ceiling drywall.

Sill Plate

In most cases, the typical 2x6 or 2x8 sill plate can be replaced with a 2x4 plate. Sill plates can, in fact, be eliminated completely if the foundation wall is sufficiently level and metal straps are embedded in the foundation for floor anchorage. Straps are located so that they can be nailed to joists every 6 feet.

Rim (or Band) Joist

Generally, rim joists do not serve a structural function but rather provide temporary bracing for floor joists before application of the subfloor. They also help distribute the load of studs that do not align with floor joists. However, where wall studs bear directly over a floor joist, the typically used 2x material can be replaced with 1x material or structural sheathing.

WALLS AND PARTITIONS

24-inch Stud Spacing

The use of 24-inch spacing of 2x4 studs in wall framing is generally acceptable for single-story construction and for two-story construction when supported by an engineering analysis. When 2x6 studs are used to accommodate thicker insulation, they should always be acceptable for 24-inch spacing. A substantial savings in both labor and materials can be realized. Thermal bridging is also reduced.

Single Top Plate

The primary function of a double top plate is to distribute nonaligning loads. Where roof trusses align with wall studs and transfer their load directly, a single top plate is acceptable. A single top plate can also be used in all nonload-bearing interior partition walls. Single top plates can be spliced with a steel "truss" plate or by the use of a splice block.

Corner Posts and Partition Posts

Two studs are all that is required where two walls intersect at corners; however, most builders use at least three studs and spacer blocking. Similarly, a single stud is adequate where one wall abuts another; however, most builders use a three-stud "partition post." The extra studs are nonstructural nailers for interior finishing. With two-stud corners and one-stud partition posts, back-up for interior finish materials can be provided by either metal clips or plywood cleats spaced 2 feet apart.

Window and Door Headers

Structural headers are generally not required in nonload-bearing walls, although it is important to check with local building officials in high-wind areas. Jack studs are not required for openings in nonload-bearing walls.

In load-bearing walls, structural box beams can replace solid headers in some cases. Structural box beams are suitable for openings up to 6 feet wide in houses up to 28 feet in depth where the headers carry either floor loads or roof loads, but not both. The total design load cannot exceed 500 pounds per lineal foot over the beam. Structural box beams, made by glue-nailing structural sheathing to 2x framing material, also provide a cavity for insulation (Figure 22). Refer to *Cost-Effective Home Building* for more details.

Let-in Bracing

Depending on the local jurisdiction, let-in bracing can provide the required racking strength in exterior walls. Also, some local jurisdictions permit the use of metal tension straps to provide the required racking strength. in these cases, the straps are typically installed diagonally in both directions.

Nonload-bearing Interior Partition Walls

For these walls, 2x3 studs at 24 inches on center with single top plates can be used; all headers and jack studs can be eliminated.

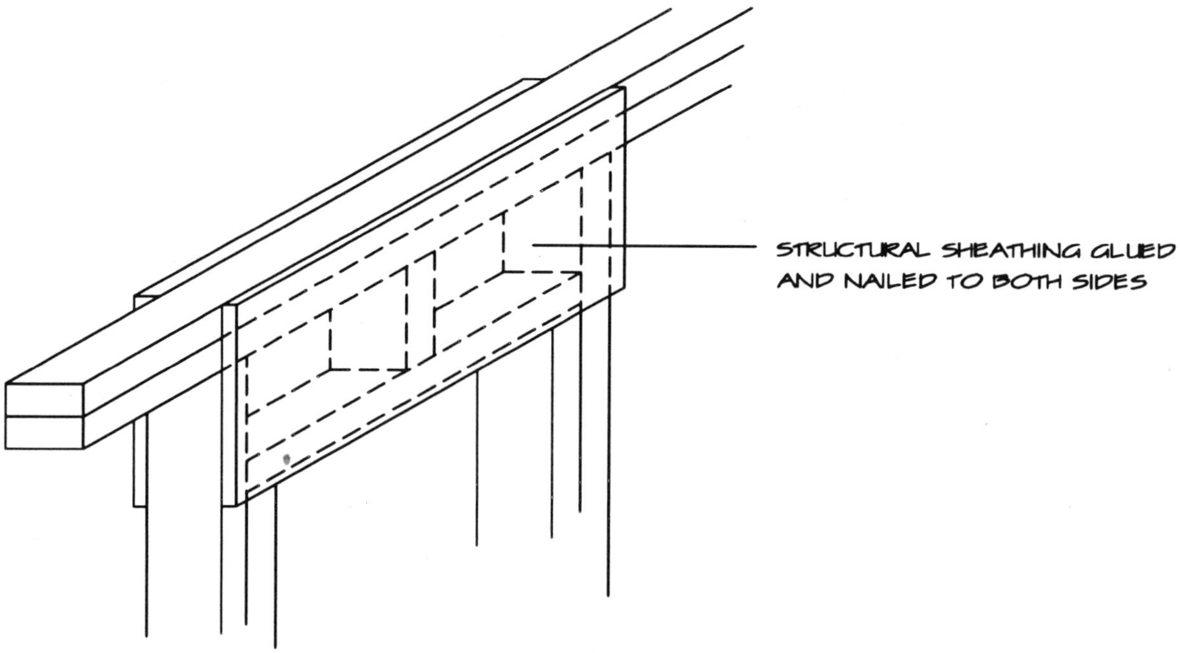

Figure 22. Structural Box Beam

INFORMATION SOURCE

Additional information about frost-protected shallow foundations can be obtained from:

NAHB Research Center
400 Prince George's Boulevard
Upper Marlboro, MD 20772
(800) 638-8556

Summary Recommendations for Alternatives to Lumber and Plywood

The literature reviews conducted in preparing this book identified a variety of methods and materials that reduce the amount of lumber and plywood used in residential construction. Alternative materials that are readily available include engineered wood products, laminated fiberboard structural sheathing, steel framing, concrete systems and concrete block, foam core panels, and plastic.

Engineered wood products (EWP) and steel are common construction materials employed as typical 16- or 24-inch on center framing. EWPs also can be used as a structural sheathing material. Further, steel can be used in homes for interior partition wall framing and is familiar to most drywall contractors.

Even though concrete systems and concrete block can reduce the amount of wood in a home, their use usually requires the additional step of furring to accommodate the finish materials preferred by most home buyers. In addition, utility systems may have to be rerouted or installed in chases.

Foam core panels offer an entire assembly that replaces the exterior wall or roof, not merely the individual framing members. Foam core panels do not necessitate additional steps for applying interior finish material. However, they require careful planning and preparation for the installation of utilities.

Several emerging materials represent potential future alternatives to wood. These include additional engineered wood products and light-weight concrete. Even plastic is beginning to find use as a lumber alternative. However, the application of plastic for structural purposes is still undergoing development, and the available products are limited for use as decking, fences, and trim. Additional evaluation and testing of these products will be necessary before they become available for structural application in residential construction.

It should be noted that most of the alternatives discussed in this report currently have higher initial costs than wood yet offer advantages such as increased thermal efficiency, fire resistance, or durability. One obvious exception is oriented strand board, which currently offers cost advantages. Some of the other products could become more cost-competitive if their structural properties were fully used. For example, the longer spans made possible by some EWPs could result in the elimination of columns, beams, or other intermediate supports. It is expected that increases in lumber prices will continue. As a result, more alternatives are likely to become cost-competitive.